Renegade Gospel

The Rebel Jesus

RENEGADE GOSPEL
THE REBEL JESUS

Book
978-1-4267-9279-3
978-1-4267-9280-9 eBook

DVD
978-1-4267-9282-3

Leader Guide
978-1-4267-9281-6
978-1-63088-037-8 eBook

Youth Study Book
978-1-4267-9283-0
978-1-4267-9284-7 eBook

Children's Leader Guide
978-1-4267-9285-4

For more information, visit www.MikeSlaughter.com

Also by Mike Slaughter

Dare to Dream
shiny gods
Christmas Is Not Your Birthday
Change the World
Spiritual Entrepreneurs
Real Followers
Momentum for Life
UnLearning Church
Upside Living in a Downside Economy

Praise for *Renegade Gospel*

"We've had the sweet Jesus, Jesus as soother of hurt feelings and all-affirming therapist, Jesus as a technique to get whatever it is we think we must have. Now Mike Slaughter presents the biblical, renegade Jesus. Who better than Mike, renegade pastor that he is, to present Jesus in all of his unmanageable, demanding, troublemaking glory?"

–**Will Willimon**, United Methodist Bishop, retired; Professor
of the Practice of Christian Ministry, Duke Divinity School

"If you're a churchgoer or not, if you lean conservative or liberal, if you vote Republican or Democrat, if you're a fervent believer or a wondering skeptic… Mike Slaughter will challenge you and inspire you. I know, because that's what he does for me. *Renegade Gospel* is Mike's life and message distilled into one pure, powerful, delicious, nourishing jolt."

–**Brian D. McLaren**, Author/speaker (brianmclaren.net)

"Nothing short of a call to join God's revolution, and to rebel against everything in this world that is out of sync with God's dream for it. This isn't your grandma's Sunday school curriculum…this is a call to a holy uprising."

–**Shane Claiborne**, Author/activist

"Mike Slaughter's life, witness, and ministry are marked by two commitments: freedom, by God's grace and mercy, from subservience and acquiescence to the 'kingdoms of this world'; and radical allegiance to the reign of God unleashed in the life, death, and resurrection of Jesus Christ. Thanks be to God for this rebel who is still sold out to the Rebel."

–**Gregory Vaughn Palmer**, Resident Bishop, Ohio West
Episcopal Area, The United Methodist Church

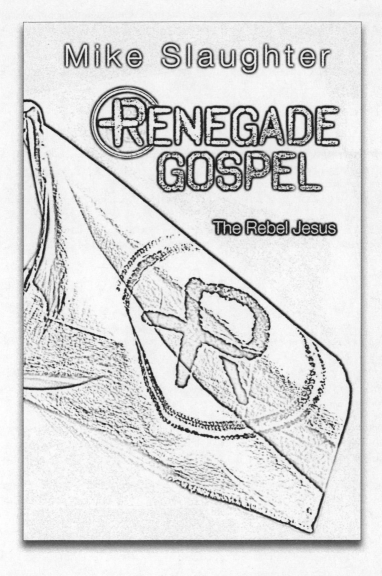

Mike Slaughter

RENEGADE GOSPEL

The Rebel Jesus

Abingdon Press / Nashville

RENEGADE GOSPEL: The Rebel Jesus

Library of Congress Cataloging-in-Publication Data

Slaughter, Michael.
   Renegade gospel : the rebel Jesus / Mike Slaughter.
      1 online resource.
   Includes bibliographical references.
   Description based on print version record and CIP data provided by publisher; resource not viewed.
   ISBN 978-1-4267-9280-9 (epub) -- ISBN 978-1-4267-9279-3 (binding: pbk., adhesive-perfect binding : alk. paper) 1. Jesus Christ--Person and offices. I. Title.
   BT203
   232--dc23

                              2014041061

This book is printed on elemental chlorine-free paper.

14 15 16 17 18 19 20 21 22 23—10 9 8 7 6 5 4 3 2 1
MANUFACTURED IN THE UNITED STATES OF AMERICA

To our newest grandson,
Caleb Michael Leavitt

CONTENTS

INTRODUCTION

"Dad, is Christianity true?"

Our two children posed this question to their mother and me sometime in that adolescent phase between the innocence of childhood belief and the challenge of adult faith.

"Jesus is truth," I emphatically stated. "But Christianity as we know it is a fallible, institutional representation of that truth."

Let's be honest. Most of us have taken the Jesus of history and recreated him in our own cultural, political, ideological, theological, and denominational bubble. This is so easy to do. We see through the lens of our family origins and cultural experiences. The great art galleries of Europe reveal centuries of humanity's cultural prejudices in projecting onto Jesus personal, nationalistic, political, and racial identities. Many in my own country, the United States, have created a partisan Jesus who sides with their own political interests. This heresy has mimicked the same mean-spiritedness and divisiveness that have been recently demonstrated by the immobilized U.S. Congress. And Jesus said his followers would be known by their love? For some, unbridled capitalism and the gospel of Jesus have been enmeshed to be representative of one and the same. And Jesus said his followers would bring good news to the poor?

In the comfort of our well-appointed sanctuaries and the security of our doctrines, we forget that Jesus was a member of a marginalized and persecuted minority. He spent the first two years of his life as a refugee in Africa due to the campaign of genocide initiated by King Herod. His mission was seen as heretical by the religiously correct and as subversive by the Roman political forces that occupied Palestine. Tradition tells us that all his disciples, except the Apostle John who died in exile on the Island of Patmos, suffered martyrs' deaths for their allegiance to this man and his mission. They were convinced he was Lord (the ultimate authority) above all other religious and political systems in the world. Their unwavering allegiance was based on their firm conviction that he was raised bodily from the dead.

I am writing this book during the season of Lent. There is no better time in the Christian year to reexamine our response to Jesus' invitation, "Come, follow me" (Matthew 4:19). It doesn't take much simply to profess our belief in Jesus. But it is a far different matter to take seriously the words of the One who tells us, "Whoever wants to be my disciple must deny themselves and take up their cross daily and follow me" (Luke 9:23). His words to the wealthy young entrepreneur haunt me in the comfort of my lifestyle: "If you want to be perfect, go, sell your possessions and give to the poor, and you will have treasure in heaven. Then come, follow me" (Matthew 19:21). I don't want to deny these radical demands of Jesus through a rationalized religiosity. The wealthy young man had no option. He stood face to face with the rebel Jesus, not a lesser creation of his Christianized imagination. So he turned and walked away deflated, choosing the comforts of wealth over the demands of discipleship.

Discipleship doesn't begin with one's profession of faith. Discipleship begins in the commitment to journey with Jesus. My friend Will Willimon with his colleague Stanley Hauerwas stated it so succinctly in their book, *Resident Aliens*:

> Early Christians, interestingly, began not with creedal speculation about the metaphysics of the Incarnation—that is, Christology abstracted from the Gospel accounts. They began with stories about Jesus, about those whose lives got caught up in his life. Therefore, in a more sophisticated and engaging way, by the very form of their presentation, the Gospel writers were able to begin training us to situate our lives like his life. We cannot know Jesus without following Jesus. Engagement with Jesus, as the misconceptions of his first disciples show, is necessary to understand Jesus. In a sense, we follow Jesus *before* we know Jesus.[1]

The Lenten season is a sobering reminder that the journey with Jesus leads to a cross. Jesus reminded the crowds that showed up motivated by self-interest, miracles of healing, and free food to count the cost of discipleship (Luke 14:25-33). He concluded by saying, "In the same way, those of you who do not give up everything you have cannot be my disciples" (verse 33).

I will be sixty-three when this book is published and a serious Jesus follower for over forty years. I have to deal, on a daily basis, with the luring sirens of materialism, the lustful passions of appetite, and the blinding comforts of living in that small percentage of privilege, in a world where a child dies every four seconds from a hunger-related cause. If you're finding it difficult to be who God needs you to be and who your family believes you to be, know that you are not alone in your struggle.

I look forward to continuing this journey with you. Together we will dare to dispel the illusions about a benign Savior who only taught us nice ways to live, who lives eternally to serve our personal needs and then takes us to heaven when we die. Jesus is so much more than this! Let's rediscover the rebel who came to initiate the radical movement of God that will "bring good news to the poor, ... bind up the broken-hearted, ... [and] proclaim release for captives" (Isaiah 61:1 CEB).

CHAPTER ONE
DISCOVERING THE REBEL JESUS

Chapter One
Discovering the Rebel Jesus

Jesus answered,
"I am the way and the truth and the life."
(John 14:6)

Growing up in Cincinnati, Ohio, in the 1950s, I attended with my parents what I call the First Church of the Frozen Chosen. The people at my church didn't talk much about Jesus. They would talk about God, about dying and going to heaven, and once in awhile about the stories of the Sunday school Jesus, a Jesus I often pictured as a benign white male with shiny long hair, red lips, and perhaps a big heart on his chest. Only a handful of people at my childhood church demonstrated a passionate enthusiasm about Jesus that made an impact on how they lived their lives that was noticeable enough to mark them as somehow different in my eight-year-old eyes. As a result, I saw Jesus as no more than

Warner Sallman's famous "Head of Christ" painting that hung on the church wall—hardly a real person at all, much less a radical or a rebel.

It was then that I started to glimpse a picture of a Jesus I could follow.

By the time I was an upperclassmen in high school, during the early days of the Jesus movement, some credible disciples of Christ started to get my attention. John Perkins, a Civil Rights leader, community developer, and preacher in Jackson, Mississippi, was willing to be beaten and jailed for his beliefs. Tom Skinner, a former African American gang leader in Harlem, discovered the rebel Jesus and became the co-founder of the National Black Evangelical Association, an organization dedicated—as fellow believers with white Christians—to challenging white evangelical institutions to address critical injustices such as racism, hunger, and poverty. Juan Carlos Ortiz, born in the jungles of Argentina to an alcoholic father, encountered the rebel Jesus with the help of two missionaries and then founded churches in difficult urban areas like the heart of Buenos Aires, before expanding his ministry worldwide. Tony Campolo, later the author of *Red Letter Christians: A Citizen's Guide to Faith and Politics*[1] grabbed my attention as a diehard Jesus follower with a keen focus on addressing social issues that beleaguered the poor and downtrodden. It was then that I started to glimpse a picture of a Jesus I could respect, a Jesus I could follow.

That's the problem for most people—the depiction of Jesus is not contagious. Where does the problem lie? In the words of Pogo Possum from the long-running daily American comic strip *Pogo*, "We have met the enemy and he is us."[2] Many of us who claim to be Jesus followers have lost our passion, our first love for Christ. So it is not surprising that the fastest-growing religion in

America right now is "no religion." In 2012 the Pew Research Institute's research revealed:

> One-fifth of the U.S. public—and a third of adults
> under 30—are religiously unaffiliated today. . . . In the
> last five years alone, the unaffiliated have increased
> from just over 15% to just under 20% of all U.S. adults.
> Their ranks now include more than 13 million self-
> described atheists and agnostics (nearly 6% of the U.S.
> public), as well as nearly 33 million people who say
> they have no particular religious affiliation (14%).[3]

Also, Islam has become increasingly popular in the U.S., while the commitment to Christianity has declined. During a recent trip to Philadelphia to visit our son and his family, my wife, Carolyn, and I met our hotel housekeeper, a twenty-something young woman whose head was covered with the traditional hijab of the Muslim faith. She told us that even though she was born in the U.S., she was a recent convert to Islam. I have no desire to belittle Islam, but I turned to Carolyn and said, "What is it about the gospel that is so unattractive to young people that they are choosing other religions, feeling that they offer more hope?" A better question might have been, "What is it about Christians that is so unappealing?"

I think we have part of the answer. We have dumbed down what it means to be a disciple of Jesus Christ. Our churches consist of members who have little to do with following Jesus. We have turned *church* into a noun, a stationary building that we visit once a week (or maybe once a month for many of us), instead of a living, functioning, working community of Jesus-following believers. The church has redefined *faithfulness* as simply showing up for worship, making a donation, and then going back home to our regular lives.

Instead of being disciples who demonstrate an undiluted devotion to Jesus as Lord, we have domesticated and watered down Jesus' true identity. We have turned faith into easy believe-ism. That's not the gospel for which John Perkins, Tom Skinner, and Juan Carlos Ortiz were willing to place their lives and reputations on the line.

A SUBVERSIVE MOVEMENT

The renegade gospel espoused by Jesus was a subversive movement. Christianity was outlawed for the first three centuries of the church. Tens of thousands of followers who publicly declared their faith were executed in coliseums throughout the Roman Empire. Perhaps it should be no surprise that today, the places in the world where Christianity is often growing the fastest are those countries where Christianity is still illegal and Christians are being persecuted by their governments.

I recently had the opportunity to train pastors for a week in Ho Chi Minh City, Vietnam. I was warned before I left about what could happen if government authorities discovered I was preaching Christ. Most likely, I would have been promptly expelled from the country and barred from returning. However, for the Vietnamese pastors, who had traveled in from rural regions for my teaching about the Christian faith, the risks were far greater, including the potential consequence of imprisonment. Jesus is often portrayed in our churches as a good-natured Mr. Rogers type who beckons the tired and weary to his neighborhood for a little R&R and entertainment, but these Vietnamese pastors know a rebel Jesus who is very different from our Sunday school Jesus.

Christians have done more to destroy the image and message of Jesus than all the atheists and agnostics combined! We are making converts to "no religion" on atheists' behalf. We must come to terms with the true nature of the rebel Jesus and acknowledge the radical nature of his message and mission.

I can't chastise other Christians without first taking a hard look at myself. Have I become too comfortable? Have I fallen into the spiritual poverty of wealth? I need to keep myself on the path of discovering the real Jesus, the true Jesus, and not the Jesus of my imagination. This isn't a journey that should stop just because I have reached a certain pinnacle or point on the trip. The journey is independent of life stage and age.

My initial discovery of the real Jesus started in the summer of 1967, before my junior year of high school, when for the first time I traveled with my grandparents to visit our relatives in Little Rock, Arkansas. Jesus was just a historical figure to me at the time. My childhood church certainly hadn't made the introduction for me. Because that church had a murky theology, no one had emphasized that Jesus was the physical embodiment of God. In fact, it seemed that Jesus was just another good, moral teacher alongside the Gandhis and Dr. Martin Luther Kings of the world. As far as my church was concerned, all paths to God seemed equally virtuous. To an extent, I had grown up with the message that it doesn't really matter what you believe as long as you are sincere. Of course, now I recognize that the terrorists who crashed into the World Trade Center were sincere. Sincerity does not necessarily make for a true faith journey.

I experienced a bit of culture shock in Little Rock. In Cincinnati I had attended a racially and socioeconomically diverse high school. I have a picture of me playing guitar with my garage band at a school dance, and I am the only white face in the photo. Little Rock was a place I had witnessed only on the evening news, and not in a positive light. Little Rock was home to Central High School, scene of an infamous school desegregation incident in 1957 when President Eisenhower sent federal troops to counter the Arkansas National Guard, which had been ordered by Governor Orval Faubus to prevent nine black students from entering the school.

In 1967, racism was still alive and well in Little Rock. I remember thinking to myself, "Man, this world is seriously messed up."

To my surprise, I discovered the unexpected in my first encounter with an Arkansas relative. Great Uncle Gilbert, my grandmother's brother, made a completely different impression from what I had experienced up to that time in Arkansas. Even though I only saw the man two or three times in my life, he left quite a wake behind him. Uncle Gilbert's home did not resemble the rest of Little Rock. When I visited his home, white and black people ate together at the dinner table and sipped sweet tea on the front porch together. They spoke freely and passionately about Jesus, acting as if he were a very real, active, and meaningful part of their daily existence. It was not like the rest of Little Rock at all—or typical "church" for that matter.

The summer of 1967, despite its surprises, did not immediately convert me to the rebel Jesus, but it certainly made me think about Jesus in a new light. Back at home, I still felt like a failure, struggled in school, and remained unsure where I was headed next. But the Spirit was moving. For some reason, I was compelled to pull from my bedstand the dusty childhood Bible I had received at church as a third grader, and I started to read it. Fortunately—and this had to be God-prompted—I started with the Gospels. Frankly, if I had started with Genesis my interest would have died in Leviticus, and I never would have made it through the Bible. The Jesus I encountered in Matthew, Mark, Luke, and John bore no resemblance to the fairy tale Jesus I had occasionally heard about in Sunday school. The portrait of the Jesus that emerged was that of a daring and dangerous radical. The real Jesus was pro-love and pro-peace, yet unafraid to challenge the hypocritical religious status quo regardless of consequences. When I began to discover the real Jesus, I was deeply attracted to what he had to offer and finally started to discover my life calling.

Revolutionary Teachings

I challenge you to reread, or read for the first time, the first four books of the New Testament—Matthew, Mark, Luke, and John. How is Jesus as presented in the Gospels different from your initial perception? What is Jesus as presented in the Gospels calling you to be and do? Review the red letters, those words that represent what Christ had to say during his brief three-year ministry on Planet Earth, to examine how revolutionary his teachings were, both two thousand years ago and today. Let's take a look at some of those teachings.

Once, on the Sabbath, Jesus boldly entered the synagogue at Capernaum and started teaching. Mark tells us, "the people were amazed at his teaching, because he taught them as one who had authority, not as the teachers of the law." (Mark 1:22). Jesus was then interrupted by a person possessed by an evil spirit, who cried, "What do you want with us, Jesus of Nazareth? Have you come to destroy us? I know who you are—the Holy One of God!" (verse 24). The demon made an excellent point. It clearly recognized who Jesus was but certainly would never claim to be a disciple. Yet many of us who call ourselves Christians make that mistake all the time. We claim that all you have to do is believe in Jesus and you will be saved. But even the demons believe! It's not what we "believe" that saves us; it's what we obey. When healing a paralytic at the Pool of Bethesda, Jesus directed the man: "Get up! Pick up your mat and walk" (John 5:8). Similarly, Jesus directed ten lepers in Luke 17:14 to "Go, show yourselves to the priests." The lepers were healed as they obeyed. True faith calls for a response. We will return to this topic in the next chapter.

Jesus came to Planet Earth as a peacemaker, but he was not a peacekeeper. In the incident with the demon, Jesus spoke harshly to it. " 'Be quiet!' said Jesus sternly. 'Come out of him!' The impure spirit shook the man violently and came out of him with a shriek" (Mark 1:25-26). The people were amazed at Jesus' compelling authority and boldness. In John 2, we see an example of Jesus' anger. He found that the Temple in Jerusalem had been turned into a "den of thieves," where businesses extorted the poor with exorbitant prices for birds or other animals that worshipers were forced to use for Temple offerings. To purchase animals for sacrifice, people had to convert their money to Temple currency, and the moneychangers had made it a win-lose proposition. Moneychangers won, and worshipers lost. When Jesus saw what was going on, he used a whip, turned over tables, and drove out the unscrupulous money mongers and cheats. His actions don't fit the image of a placid, domesticated Jesus, a "Jesus on a leash," or a Messiah that we can control and tame.

Jesus didn't guarantee his followers a trouble-free life.

Yet Jesus clearly didn't represent a God of violence, as we learn in Matthew 5:38-41. One of Jesus' most radical teachings replaced the "eye for an eye" justice of the Old Testament. Instead, Jesus taught that if someone punched you in the face, turn the other cheek and let your antagonist blast the other side as well. In that same passage, Jesus challenged us with powerful exercises in self-control. Roman law required a passerby to carry a Roman soldier's pack for one mile if asked, aiding in the movement of the army. Jesus said the passerby should carry the heavy pack a second mile, though only asked to go one. Likewise, those under the Roman Empire's iron rule were required to hand over their coats to Roman soldiers if directed to do so, Rome's low-cost strategy to outfit its army for winter. Jesus instructed those who were asked for their coats to hand over their shirts as well. These responses aren't intuitive or natural, and they don't serve our self-interest; nevertheless they reflect Jesus' teachings.

Jesus didn't guarantee his followers a trouble-free life. He taught hard truths and made no promises about easy living. In Luke 9:23-24, Jesus said, "Whoever wants to be my disciple must deny themselves and take up their cross daily and follow me. For whoever wants to save their life will lose it, but whoever loses their life for me will save it." Some were unwilling to pay the price. In the Gospel of Mark, we read about a rich young man who was eager to experience what Jesus was offering. When the young man asked what he must do to obtain eternal life, Jesus gave this unexpected response: "Go, sell everything you have and give to the poor, and you will have treasure in heaven. Then come, follow me" (Mark 10:21). As many other aspiring disciples would do, both during and following Jesus' ministry on earth, the man walked away.

Nineteenth-century British pastor Charles Spurgeon once noted, "There are no crown bearers in heaven that were not cross bearers on earth."[4] Dr. Martin Luther King, Jr., echoed a similar theme, noting, "Christianity has always insisted that the cross we bear precedes the crown we wear."[5] These are not feel-good messages that easily attract a crowd, nor were those that Jesus offered. In John we read that many of Jesus' disciples, after listening to Jesus' hard teachings, "turned back and no longer followed him" (John 6:66).

Claiming the rebel Jesus requires a radical reprioritization of all we deem valuable. In the case of the wealthy young man, the priorities to be reordered were money and possessions, but sometimes the demands were even greater. In Luke 14:26, Jesus warned the crowd, "If anyone comes to me and does not hate father and mother, wife and children, brothers and sisters—yes, even their own life—such a person cannot be my disciple." The rebel Jesus also requires reprioritization of our relationships. Certainly Jesus does not want me to "hate" Carolyn, my wife of forty-two years, or my children. Yet he makes it abundantly evident that my allegiance to him as Lord must supersede all else—and everyone else—in my life. Frankly, I am a far better husband to Carolyn than I would be otherwise when I make my relationship with Jesus the top priority.

Jesus delivered powerful teachings that were often difficult to listen to and even more challenging to live out. The Pharisees of Jesus' day were strict observers of the law that was detailed in the Old Testament, which they had subdivided into 613 separate rules supplemented with more than 1,500 additional "do's and don'ts" for living a fully righteous life. Yet Jesus at times dared to interpret the law even more strictly than the most legalistic Pharisees of the day. We find several examples of this in the Sermon on the Mount. In Matthew 5:21-22, Jesus equates anger with murder:

> "You have heard that it was said to the people long ago, 'You shall not murder, and anyone who murders will be subject to judgment.' But I tell you that anyone who is angry with a brother or sister will be subject to judgment. Again, anyone who says to a brother or sister, 'Raca,' is answerable to the court. And anyone who says, 'You fool!' will be in danger of the fire of hell."

Next, in Matthew 5:27-28, Jesus tackled adultery and divorce stating: "You have heard that it was said, 'You shall not commit adultery.' But I tell you that anyone who looks at a woman lustfully has already committed adultery with her in his heart." Jesus then redefined the acceptable grounds for divorce previously allowed within the Law and practiced by its most diligent adherents: "It has been said, 'Anyone who divorces his wife must give her a certificate of divorce.' But I tell you that anyone who divorces his wife, except for sexual immorality, makes her the victim of adultery, and anyone who marries a divorced woman commits adultery" (verses 31-32).

Many more of Jesus' teachings conflicted with what the self-righteously religious of Jesus' time would have believed or practiced, and they certainly run counter to what our contemporary world embraces and promotes: "love your neighbor as yourself" (Matthew 22:39); "the last will be first, and the first will be last" (Matthew 20:16); "the Son of Man did not come to be served, but to serve" (Matthew 20:28); "unless you change and become like little children, you will never enter the kingdom of heaven" (Matthew 18:3). Jesus could never be perceived as a protector of the status quo. Even the Beatitudes, which open the Sermon on the Mount, can be considered controversial or even undesirable. Yes, you are blessed—*if* you mourn, are meek, are poor in spirit, and so on. After reading the list, one might be inclined to say, "I never want to be that blessed!"

The night before Jesus' execution, he was arrested in the garden of Gethsemane right after the Last Supper. His disciple Peter drew a sword, swung it, and sliced the ear off one of the soldiers. Jesus told Peter to put the sword away, saying that "all who draw the sword will die by the sword" (Matthew 26:52). Then, in the following verse, Jesus made this incredible statement: "Do you think I cannot call on my Father, and he will at once put at my disposal more than twelve legions of angels?" If I were in Jesus' shoes and had twelve legions of angels at my command, I would have been singing right along with Twisted Sister, "Oh, we're not gonna take it anymore." But Jesus never played that card, because he chose for mercy to trump vengeance. Nailed to the cross, soldiers gambling for his clothes, people hurling insults and mocking him, Jesus prayed, "Father, forgive them, for they do not know what they are doing" (Luke 23:34). Instead of destroying his enemies, Jesus chose to give his life to save the mockers and the persecutors. The cross was Jesus' most radical demonstration of God's kingdom.

HIGH STANDARDS, WITH GRACE

In fact, the key difference between Jesus and the Pharisees was not their often-shared ideals but Jesus' insistence on grace. Yes, Jesus challenged the disciples then, and still calls followers today, to pursue seemingly impossible standards. As Peter reminds us, "But just as he who called you is holy, so be holy in all you do" (1 Peter 1:15). So, despite never lowering the standard, grace triumphed. Peter himself is a perfect example. After he denied Jesus three times during one of the blackest hours on the darkest day of Christ's earthly life, Jesus completely forgave Peter, restored him, and then used him as a key builder of the early church. Jesus extended grace and forgiveness to the criminal on the cross and, even less understandably, to the jeering crucifiers at his feet below as he died.

Although Jesus always called his followers to enter the small gate and take the narrow road to the Kingdom, he repeatedly taught mercy and relationship over rigidity and judgment. Consider the people who caught Jesus' attention during his ministry on Planet Earth. They included a poor widow with two small coins, a hemorrhaging woman, lepers, the blind, an unnamed child, an adulteress, prostitutes, and a short, thieving tax collector who clambered up a tree to grab a glimpse of Jesus walking by. As I read about these encounters in my boyhood Bible during my late teens, I began to realize that I needed a God who looked like Jesus.

The teachings of Jesus spoke authoritatively to me as I read the Gospels each night in my bedroom. His teachings started movements. His teachings changed the world, sometimes even through non-Christian agents. Gandhi practiced the nonviolent teachings of Christ to overthrow the British Empire in India. Dr. Martin Luther King, Jr., a devout follower of Christ, practiced the same nonviolent teachings to start the U.S. down the long, difficult path toward civil rights; it wasn't the often-militant tactics of the Black Panther Party, as some might argue, that got the job done. Every night I found myself reading my Bible; I couldn't put it down. The red letters were too compelling. Finally I said to Jesus, "I don't even know if you are real, but if you are, I need you."

Now, Jesus didn't leave me there. He had far bigger, more radical plans, a calling for my life that almost everyone who had watched me grow up found hilarious or at least ironic. After encountering the real Jesus, I realized I was called to be a minister. And being a minister meant I had years of education in front of me—the last thing I had wanted to pursue in my life given my academic record. Fortunately, Jesus repeatedly extended the grace I needed to make fulfillment of my call possible.

FOUR NAMES OF JESUS

As I continued to explore the Gospels throughout my college years and the unique attraction of the true, radical Jesus, I also began to uncover and study the four names by which Jesus is frequently identified in Scripture—four identities that are both compelling and challenging: Son of God, Son of Man, Servant of All, and Savior of the World.

Jesus as Son of God carries the genetic code, the DNA, of God the Father. Jesus is a chip off the old block, so to speak, serving as a visible picture of a God who otherwise would be invisible. Jesus is the exact representation of God's being and the living expression of the Father's heart. Jesus took religion out of the synagogue and Temple and made it accessible to all. As you read the Gospels, note how often Jesus taught from hillsides, homes, and boats, not just in the pulpit. He boldly demonstrated that a building wasn't required, proclaiming in John 14:6 that "I am the way and the truth and the life. No one comes to the Father except through me." Of course, far too often religious folks have used that proclamation as a fence or border to define who is in and who is out. But I don't believe that was Jesus' intent. He was saying, in effect, "You will never know the love of God as a parent except through me." Through Jesus, God no longer appears as the holy, untouchable judge but instead as the ultimate parent who loves us powerfully and intimately.

The second name, Son of Man, is the way Jesus referred to himself. If Jesus as Son of God reveals God the Father, then Jesus as Son of Man enables us to see our true selves, our "child-of-God selves" (John 1:12, *The Message*). We can begin to see ourselves as God does and embrace our own value, possibilities, and potential.

We forget to live the life that Jesus promised now and to live it abundantly.

In the church we celebrate two major holidays, Easter and Christmas. As I currently write this book, I am practicing the repentance and discipline of Lent. I am looking forward to the celebration of the Resurrection and the reaffirmation that Jesus considered me valuable enough to die for. Christmas, of course, embodies the miracle of Incarnation, when God became a human being: "The Word became flesh and blood, and moved into the neighborhood" (John 1:14, *The Message*). So much of institutional Christianity and other world religions, for that matter, involve a denial or demeaning of our humanness. Too often we in the church focus on escaping this corrupted flesh and going to heaven. We live as if we are to trudge our way begrudgingly through this world while awaiting our opportunity for heaven later. In doing so, we forget to live the life that Jesus promised now and to live it abundantly (John 10:10).

So many of us have body image problems. We look at our humanness and don't like the way we look or smell. We are embarrassed about who we are. But Jesus as Son of Man was born as a vulnerable baby. God thought you and I were so incredible that he came to Planet Earth to live life as one of us. That's powerful. That attracts me to Jesus, who calls us to embrace the possibilities of what it means to be human beings. In John 14:12 Jesus assures his disciples that "whoever believes in me will do the works I have been doing." In other words, don't waste your life, don't be afraid, step out, take risks. Jesus, the Son of Man, calls us to celebrate life as a holy gift.

Jesus' third name is Servant of All. I find this image of Jesus compelling, as it reminds me that in serving Jesus' radical plan of loving the world, I experience God and the transformation of my own life. In Matthew 20:28, Jesus said that "the Son of Man did not come to be served, but to serve, and to give his life as a ransom for many." The Kingdom that the rebel Jesus represents is in stark contrast to a secular culture that propagates the destructive myths of materialism and accumulation. In my forty-plus years of following Jesus, the times when I have felt closest to God and the deepest thrill in living have been when I have served with other brothers and sisters as Jesus' hands, feet, and voice in the world. When we follow Jesus and serve God's purpose, life explodes with meaning.

Jesus' fourth name is Savior of the World. Jesus, as savior and peacemaker, came so that we and the world might experience true peace. The Apostle Paul reminds us in Philippians 4:5-7:

> The Lord is near. Do not be anxious about anything,
> but in every situation, by prayer and petition, with

thanksgiving, present your requests to God. And the peace of God, which transcends all understanding, will guard your hearts and your minds in Christ Jesus.

In Colossians 1:19-20, Paul confirms Christ's role as peace-bringer: "For God was pleased to have all his fullness dwell in him, and through him to reconcile to himself all things, whether things on earth or things in heaven, by making peace through his blood, shed on the cross." Following the rebel Jesus does not ensure happiness. Happiness is elusive and based on our living within perfect circumstances, and how often does that happen? Jesus does not guarantee a perfect life, but he does promise peace.

Frankly, I need the peace that Jesus brings. I consider myself a pro-life pacifist. I don't support abortion or capital punishment, believing matters of life and death belong in God's hands alone, not mine. I struggle with the need for war and find torture abhorrent. But I remember my sense of overwhelming and blinding outrage when thousands of innocents were killed on September 11, 2001. I know how easily I see red and am ready to strangle with my own bare hands if someone wrongs Carolyn or one of my kids. I have had moments in which every pacifist cell in my body instead cries out for judgment, Old Testament style, an eye for an eye, a pound for a pound, a blow for a blow. Thank God I have Jesus as savior and peacemaker in my life to pull me up short. Jesus reminds me that God demands none of my blood for my failures, my screw-ups, my sin. Instead, through the rebel Jesus, God offered his own blood in place of mine. Because of that, you and I can deeply experience that peace with God that passes all human understanding.

Jesus did not come to start a religion. I doubt that he ever said to himself, "Okay, now I am going to begin something called

Christianity." Instead, the rebel Jesus came with a renegade gospel to start a revolution that would be propelled by a countercultural community of people on Planet Earth. And you and I are invited to be a part.

Before you continue with the next chapter, I encourage you to pull out your Bible and choose just one of the Gospels. Read the red letters; discover Jesus all over again, or for the very first time. Then get ready for a roller-coaster ride. In the next chapter, we will tackle what it means to live a revolutionary lifestyle when we get serious about Jesus, the real Jesus, and not the Jesus of our imagination.

CHAPTER TWO
REVOLUTIONARY LIFESTYLE

CHAPTER TWO
REVOLUTIONARY LIFESTYLE

They will rebuild the ancient ruins
and restore the places long devastated;
they will renew the ruined cities
that have been devastated for generations.
(Isaiah 61:4)

A USA Today article from May 2012 reported on a survey of
a thousand Protestant pastors. Not surprisingly, the poll
revealed that Mother's Day ranked right after Easter and Christmas
in peak church attendance. The article went on to note, "Father's
Day, however, is near the bottom of the poll although both holidays
were founded as church events more than a century ago."[1] During
my thirty-five years at Ginghamsburg Church, just north of Dayton, Ohio, this has certainly proved true. On Mother's Day we fill
every seat in the worship center and usually have to set up extras.

But annually, Father's Day proves to be one of our least attended weekends. Mothers bring their families to church on their special day; fathers tend to hit the links. Studies throughout the past decade have varied slightly in findings, but most of them show men composing approximately 39 percent of worshiping communities.

In the twentieth and twenty-first centuries, the church has strayed far away from our roots as a subversive movement under radical leadership.

Although multiple factors come into play, I believe part of men's absence is attributable to the current image of Jesus we present to the world, a domesticated and docile Jesus, a Jesus who is perfect for tea with Grannie but not much of a man, much less a God who is powerful, confrontational when necessary, and oftentimes dangerous. In the twentieth and twenty-first centuries, the church has strayed far away from our roots as a subversive movement under radical leadership. A few years ago, an article in *The Christian Century* asked the question "Why do men stay away?" Although multiple theories were touted, the author concluded that the best clue could be found within the Eastern Orthodox Church, a church that was attracting men and women in more equal numbers. The author pointed out that religion journalist Frederica Mathewes-Green "surveyed male adult converts and discovered that Orthodoxy's main appeal is that it's 'challenging.' One convert said, 'Orthodoxy is serious. It is difficult. It is demanding. It is about mercy, but it is also about overcoming myself.' Another said that he was sick of 'bourgeois, feel-good American Christianity.' "[2]

THE TAMING OF THE CHURCH

As mentioned in Chapter One, for the first three hundred years after Jesus' incendiary movement began, the church was illegal. This time period is frequently referred to as the "age of the martyrs," when there were ten great government-sponsored persecutions against the church, some that were spurred on by local Roman authorities and others that were Empire-wide. The last and perhaps most severe of these great persecutions was known as the Diocletianic Persecution (or Great Persecution), ordered in A.D. 303 by the Roman emperor Diocletian, who ruled from 284 to 305.

Why was Christianity so threatening to the Roman government? Converts to the faith declared, "Jesus is Lord." This simple phrase sounds innocent enough to twenty-first-century American ears; but in the Roman Empire of that time, saying "Jesus is Lord" was both heresy and treason. Under Roman law, Caesar was Lord. Caesar alone yielded absolute power and authority. In the government-sponsored persecutions, tens of thousands of believers were executed publicly, often left hanging on crosses along major roadways so that all people would witness the penalty for proclaiming Jesus as Lord. Other believers lost their lives in front of the crowds that packed Roman coliseums located throughout the empire. New Christians courageously refused to bow to the religious or political barriers that denied and defied Jesus' authority. These Christians accepted the clear and present danger of following Jesus, no matter the consequences to self or family, and many were martyred for their faith. The word *martyr* in Greek means witness, and what a witness it was, and how different from the "witness wear" and car clings we use now to express our faith.

This was the world that the Apostle Paul traveled and ministered within. Everywhere Paul journeyed on behalf of Christ, he and the church were in jeopardy and met with resistance at every turn. During Paul's second missionary journey, he stopped at a town called Thessalonica in Greece. Jason, a believer, had hosted Paul and Paul's traveling companion Silas in his home. Let's pick up the story in Acts 17:5-8.

> But other Jews were jealous; so they rounded up some bad characters from the marketplace, formed a mob and started a riot in the city. They rushed to Jason's house in search of Paul and Silas in order to bring them out to the crowd. But when they did not find them, they dragged Jason and some other believers before the city officials, shouting: "These men who have caused trouble all over the world have now come here, and Jason has welcomed them into his house. They are all defying Caesar's decrees, saying that there is another king, one called Jesus." When they heard this, the crowd and the city officials were thrown into turmoil.

"These men who have caused trouble all over the world. . . ." When did Christians stop causing trouble? When did the church become so tame? In A.D. 313, the Caesar of Rome, Constantine, issued the Edict of Milan, legalizing Christian worship. No doubt during his predecessors' rule Constantine had noted Christians' stubborn persistence in clinging to their faith and allegiance to Christ no matter what persecution they endured. Constantine perhaps realized that if he harnessed that fervor and allegiance to Rome, the Empire would prove unconquerable. From that point forward, the Christian flag would fly under the flag of Rome.

This new, legalized status for Christianity thankfully diminished the persecutions but ironically would prove to deal an almost fatal blow to the vibrancy of the church. Jesus' followers started to become comfortable and complacent. Christians enjoyed being part of the status quo instead of the rebellious fringe. In essence, Constantine made the church an instrument of the state; and in the fourth century the church started to lose the radical nature of a renegade gospel. The gospel became civilized, the rebel Jesus domesticated, and the movement institutionalized and ritualized. In the book *ReJesus: A Wild Messiah for a Missional Church*, authors Michael Frost and Alan Hirsch share a quip from an archbishop who once said, "Everywhere Jesus went there was a riot. Everywhere I go they make me cups of tea!"[3]

A KINGDOM OF GOD WORLDVIEW

Our commitment to Jesus means commitment to a revolutionary lifestyle, in which we do not subjugate our allegiance to Christ to any other priority. The commitment means ensuring that our lifestyle is in alignment with a kingdom of God worldview. A worldview is defined as a set of fundamental beliefs that determine primary life values, decisions, and actions. The contemporary world embraces numerous worldviews—capitalist, communist, socialist, democratic, just to name a few. New Testament Scripture uses the Greek word cosmos to represent this concept of worldview. Actually, cosmos may be defined in one of three ways within its scriptural context. First, cosmos may be used in Scripture simply to denote Planet Earth. Second, cosmos at times refers to humans, or the diverse group of human beings that occupy the planet. However, the third usage of cosmos denotes any system that is not under the authority of God or part of God's kingdom. This third type of cosmos, or worldview, is considered evil and is defined as a system of evil ruled by ungodly forces. The Apostle John is referring to this usage of cosmos (translated here as "world") in 1 John 2:15 when he warns Christians: "Do not love the world or anything in the world. If anyone loves the world, love for the Father is not in them." Clearly John is not referring to the planet that God created or the people for whom God was willing to experience a brutal death on the cross.

Systems that lie outside the authority of God are in essence heresies. By marrying the Christian faith with the Roman Empire, Constantine—intentionally or not—launched the heresy of the nation state. This heresy meant that Christians began to value, honor, and prioritize a worldly system, ideology, and politics over the kingdom of God. Jesus' authority began to be subjugated to the state's authority. "For God and country" became the rallying cry for Christians instead of "Jesus is Lord."

The heresy of the nation state is why Ginghamsburg Church, the United Methodist Church where I have served as pastor for more than thirty-five years, does not fly the American flag on any of our campuses. We respect and appreciate the advantages of the democracy in which we live, but our allegiance to God's kingdom must supersede our allegiance to the nation state. Avoiding this heresy means that, although we desire to be law-abiding citizens, we are never to subjugate God's laws to the nation state's laws. It explains why, in just one example, many United Methodist bishops are working on behalf of immigration reform. In early 2014, bishops and other church leaders were arrested in front of the White House and in Chicago as they protested and prayed for immigration and deportation reform. These bishops are acting in accordance with God's directive, which in this case is in opposition to that of the nation state. Leviticus 19:33-34 provides one key example: "When a foreigner resides among you in your land, do not mistreat them. The foreigner residing among you must be treated as your native-born. Love them as yourself, for you were foreigners in Egypt. I am the LORD your God." Too often we as Christians are allowing MSNBC, Fox News, or talk-show pundits to become the genesis of our values, rather than looking to the kingdom, will, and word of God.

Jesus is Lord! Not the nation state.

One of my spiritual heroes is Dietrich Bonhoeffer (1906-1945), a powerful example of a Jesus follower who would not accommodate the values of the Kingdom to the laws and values of the nation state. Bonhoeffer was a German Lutheran pastor and theologian who helped found the Confessing Church, a group organized to resist Nazi efforts to co-opt the German Protestant church. Bonhoeffer also was an anti-Nazi dissident, publicly criticizing Adolf Hitler's regime in his writings and sermons and even in a radio message that was switched off the air before its conclusion. He boldly asserted, "Leaders of offices which set themselves up as gods mock God."[4] The U.S. Holocaust Memorial Museum's website describes Bonhoeffer as "one of the few church leaders who stood in courageous opposition to the Fuehrer [Adolf Hitler] and his policies."[5] Bonhoeffer's outspoken opposition through both word and deed led to his martyrdom—death by hanging—in the Flossenbürg concentration camp in 1945, just days before Germany's surrender to the Allied forces. Remember, the word *martyr* comes from the root word *witness*, and what a witness Bonhoeffer was. Jesus is Lord! Not the nation state. Dietrich Bonhoeffer gave his life in demonstration of that priority.

A second heresy we must avoid in a revolutionary lifestyle is that of a privatized faith. When we privatize our faith, we cease to be salt and light in the world. No longer part of a countercultural revolution, or an outpost of heaven demonstrating God's plan for restoration and resurrection, we reduce our faith to this: "Jesus came, died, and rose from the grave to get me into heaven." No! We don't pray to get to heaven; we actively pray and work to get the kingdom of heaven into earth. In the Gospel of Luke (4:18-19), Jesus quoted Isaiah 61:1 as his mission statement:

> The Spirit of the Sovereign LORD is on me,
>> because the LORD has anointed me
>> to proclaim good news to the poor.
> He has sent me to bind up the brokenhearted,
>> to proclaim freedom for the captives
>> and release from darkness for the prisoners.

Isaiah 61 goes on to remind us in verse 4 that God's people are to "rebuild the ancient ruins and restore the places long devastated; they will renew the ruined cities that have been devastated for generations." Salvation, of course, is personal, but it's also social. It is heresy when the church makes it all about one while ignoring the other. If we focus only on the social, or our ministry and mission toward others, we lack the power of the new birth and the filling of the Holy Spirit that are critical for bringing about true and lasting change. If we make it privatized, or only personal, the church fails to rebuild, restore, and renew.

Sometimes we use a focus on privatized faith to make ourselves an exception to Jesus' call for sacrificial service, mission, and giving. We assume that some of Jesus' mandates do not apply to us. I call this "design a religion" or "cafeteria theology." We practice "self-authority" in our chosen lifestyle instead of submitting to Jesus as Lord. This form of privatized faith is not an option the rebel Jesus leaves us: "Whoever wants to be my disciple must deny themselves and take up their cross daily and follow me. For whoever wants to save their life will lose it, but whoever loses their life for me will save it" (Luke 9:23-24).

My wife, Carolyn, and I almost fell into this trap during the twentieth year of our marriage. We were leading emotionally separate lives; our marriage was a travesty. In our thoughts and conversations we had begun to entertain the "easy out" of divorce. Yet, based on the authority of Jesus, this option could not be on the table for two people who claimed Jesus as the Lord of our lives. We rejected our self-authority, turned to Jesus' absolute authority, and recommitted to our marriage, which has grown stronger year after year since we course-corrected our allegiance.

Revelation 21:1 holds the promise of a new heaven and a new earth when Jesus returns. Then the community of believers will be part of a new *polis*, a Greek word meaning city or body of citizens. We are designed to live and be in community, all vital parts of the same body. All of us—all the parts—are needed to present the full array of spiritual gifts that Paul so eloquently describes in 1 Corinthians 12. People today love to claim they are spiritual but not religious. What they are implying is, "I do not need to be part of the body of believers. I can do this alone." A revolutionary lifestyle requires connection into a radical community of Jesus followers, or else we will not live into the full potential of all that the rebel Jesus has designed and called us to be.

Another Greek word used throughout the New Testament is *ekklesia*, typically translated simply as "church." However, a more accurate translation would be "the called-out ones." When we commit our lives to the rebel Jesus, we are to become part of *ekklesia*, or called-out ones, who are to form a new kingdom of God *polis* of justice. In 1 Peter 2:9 we read, "But you are a chosen people, a royal priesthood, a holy nation, God's special possession, that you may declare the praises of him who called you out of darkness into his wonderful light." In verse 5 Peter describes the community this way: "You also, like living stones, are being built into a spiritual house to be a holy priesthood, offering spiritual sacrifices acceptable to God through Jesus Christ." We are designed to live our lives together within a shared, missional community that will bring the kingdom of God to Planet Earth.

A contemporary example of what it means to create a kingdom of God *polis* as the called-out ones was in 1955 when Dr. Martin Luther King, Jr., and his team led the bus strike in Montgomery, Alabama, during the civil rights movement. Dr. King, a dedicated practitioner of nonviolence, called out African American citizens to go on strike against public transportation in protest of the discrimination that required them to take seats in the back of the bus. Those citizens participating committed to staying on strike, regardless of expense, time, or physical inconvenience. The strike was to persist until a new *polis* of justice replaced the corrupt one.

In essence, this new kind of community was what Jesus challenged us to when he said in Matthew 5:14-16:

> "You are the light of the world. A town built on a hill cannot be hidden. Neither do people light a lamp and put it under a bowl. Instead they put it on its stand, and it gives light to everyone in the house. In the same way, let your light shine before others, that they may see your good deeds and glorify your Father in heaven."

In verse 13 Jesus called us "the salt of the earth. But if the salt loses its saltiness, how can it be made salty again? It is no longer good for anything, except to be thrown out and trampled underfoot." I like to remind the people of Ginghamsburg Church that after they are baptized, their old selves are dead, buried, and out of the way, and they are fully submitted to the authority and call of Christ. If baptized believers still have preferences, excuses, or complaints about what it means to follow the rebel Jesus, then clearly we didn't hold them under the water long enough. They have ceased to be light, lost their saltiness, in the world Jesus loves.

The Authority of Jesus' Teachings

Practicing a revolutionary lifestyle means submitting ourselves fully to the authority of Jesus' teachings. In Matthew 7 Jesus shared the parable of the wise and foolish builders, stating in verses 24-25:

> "Therefore everyone who hears these words of mine and puts them into practice is like a wise man who built his house on the rock. The rain came down, the streams rose, and the winds blew and beat against that house; yet it did not fall, because it had its foundation on the rock."

Note that we not only need to hear the words of Jesus, we need to practice them. Otherwise, as with the house of the foolish builder, "'the rain came down, the streams rose, and the winds blew and beat against that house, and it fell with a great crash'" (verse 27). Jesus' audience of the day certainly found his words credible: "When Jesus had finished saying these things, the crowds were amazed at his teaching, because he taught as one who had authority, and not as their teachers of the law" (v. 28-29).

Many Christians today struggle significantly with basing their priorities and whole life practice on the authority of Jesus' teachings. In part this can be attributed to declining church attendance, in both in the U.S. and in Europe. Fewer people are hearing God's word, and no doubt even fewer are reading God's word. Even so, for those of us who do hear Jesus' teaching, many fail to practice it. Hearing without practicing yields a powerless faith.

According to the Hartford Institute for Religion Research, the U.S. and Canada have over 200 Christian denominations, with an additional 35,000 independent or nondenominational churches.[6] All confess Jesus as Lord—or rather, most profess Jesus as Lord but without the commitment to practice it as their lifestyle. This is a problem. In part, we fail to act on Jesus' teachings because, as discussed in Chapter One, the teachings are hard. Look again, for example, at Jesus' mandate on divorce and remarriage in Matthew 5:31-32. According to that passage, if Jesus is Lord, then divorce is not an option. Yet, as I look out over my congregation each weekend, I know that a significant segment of the listeners are divorced, in some cases multiple times. I am not condemning those who have divorced; sometimes it is the least bad of two terrible options, and God is the God of the do-over and second chances. Yet, if Jesus is Lord in our lives, it seems that divorce would be far less prevalent.

Jesus also reminded us frequently of our responsibility to the poor. His directive to the rich young man in the Gospel of Mark was to "sell everything you have and give to the poor" (Mark 10:21). But Christians continue to accumulate superfluous stuff, stricken by "affluenza" along with the rest of the culture. As proclaimed Jesus followers, we need to remember that we are not saved by what we believe but by what we obey. The revolutionary lifestyle requires so much more than the simplistic, easy believe-ism that we propagate within the institutional church. Jesus cautioned us about this, saying in Matthew 7:21-23:

> "Not everyone who says to me, 'Lord, Lord,' will enter the kingdom of heaven, but only the one who does the will of my Father who is in heaven. Many will say to me on that day, 'Lord, Lord, did we not prophesy in your name and in your name drive out demons and

in your name perform many miracles?' Then I will tell them plainly, 'I never knew you. Away from me, you evildoers!'"

Our works do not save us, but the fruit of our faith should be obedience to what Jesus taught. Even the demons in Scripture professed Jesus as Lord, but Jesus' mandate was not simply to believe in him but to follow him. Faith is acting on Jesus' directive to follow, which means that his lifestyle becomes our lifestyle. Our soul and sole priority are to be based on Christ's life and teachings.

In Matthew 7:13-14, Jesus told us which of the two paths we must choose: "Enter through the narrow gate. For wide is the gate and broad is the road that leads to destruction, and many enter through it. But small is the gate and narrow the road that leads to life, and only a few find it." In the church we have actually created a third way. We act as if the narrow way belongs to the pastor, the wide way to the lost, and the middle way, somewhere between the other two, to the rest of us. This is not what Jesus said. Every person who names Jesus as Lord had better be prepared to die for Jesus, be arrested for Jesus, and, yes, even live for Jesus.

The Gospel of John starts with this proclamation in 1:1: "In the beginning was the Word, and the Word was with God, and the Word was God." *Logos* is the Greek word for Jesus as the Living Word. Verse 14 continues: "The Word [Logos] became flesh and made his dwelling among us." Jesus represented the life of God fleshed out, and through Jesus the will of God was physically expressed. The Logos serves as the absolute authority on which we are to commit all our life practices and priorities. This is why the heresies of the nation state and of privatized faith are so dangerous: they do not reflect God's will as embodied in the Logos.

Jesus himself made it clear that he superseded the written word.

Now, there is a caution. We are to commit our all, our whole being, to the directive of the Logos, the Living Word, but we are not to subjugate the Logos to the *written* word. Many within the church have begun to practice Bible idolatry, acting as if the written word were the highest authority. Through the ages and continuing today, the church has used the written word as an excuse or justification for not obeying the directives of Jesus. The written word has been deployed to justify war, slavery, genocide, racism, sexism, and a whole host of other "isms" that do not reflect Kingdom values. Jesus himself made it clear that he superseded the written word. With that in mind, let's return to Matthew 5. At six points in the chapter, Jesus quoted the books of Moses or other parts of the Torah, and then he changed them. He did this in reference to murder, adultery, divorce, solemn pledges, retribution, and love. Jesus began each section with the words "You have heard that it was said," then followed with "But I say to you…." Let's look more carefully at an example.

In Matthew 5:38, Jesus said, "You have heard that it was said, 'Eye for eye and tooth for tooth.'" This expression appears in the Old Testament in Exodus 21:24, Leviticus 24:20, and Deuteronomy 19:21. Let's place this law in a contemporary setting. The church I pastor, Ginghamsburg Church, is just north of Dayton, Ohio, a city once known as a thriving center for the tool and die industry. Through the years many Ginghamsburg members have made their living as machinists in local shops. Let's say that one of those members was hurt because of defective machinery—perhaps a hand was crushed. Based on the law of "eye for eye and tooth for tooth," worker compensation would take the form of the machine shop owner's hand, or foreman's hand, being crushed as well—a just retribution. But Jesus said that that type of retribution was not God's intention. Jesus, noting that his authority superseded the authority of the written word, told his followers, "If anyone slaps you on the right cheek, turn to them the other cheek also" (Matthew 5:39). If we make the written word, the Bible, our highest authority, then much of the world would become toothless and blind! I find much in the Old Testament that does not seem to align with the teachings of Jesus, especially those passages in which God commands biblical heroes to destroy entire communities, killing all men, women, and even children. When I encounter those difficult passages, I return to the red letters, the words of Jesus found in the New Testament, and then reread the troublesome passages through the lens of Jesus.

Whenever I teach on this subject, someone inevitably will ask me, "But doesn't the New Testament say that the word of God endures forever?" In response, let's take a closer look at 1 Peter 1:23, the passage they're referring to: "For you have been born again, not of perishable seed, but of imperishable, through the living and enduring word of God." This is another example in which the English translation is inadequate to express the original Greek text. The "word" referred to as "living and enduring" in the latter part of the verse is *Logos* in the Greek—a direct reference to Jesus as the Living Word, not to the Bible as the written word. The Logos of God endures forever. When Jesus returns and the perfect comes, we will not need the Scriptures any longer. They are all truly fulfilled and perfected in Jesus.

A DANGEROUS FAITH

Christians have made the rebel Jesus into a "safe" Jesus, a Sunday school Jesus, and have stopped taking risks on behalf of the Kingdom. Since the third century, the church has moved from being a revolutionary movement to a museum for saints, much like many of the beautiful cathedrals that dot European cities. We need to become a radical, risk-taking community that once again reflects the directives of its renegade leader and passes the movement on to the next generations. Our call to a dangerous faith is one reason why I made sure my children were exposed to some of the world's hard and challenging places. When my son was a middle school student, I took him to the demilitarized zone between North and South Korea at a time when tensions were high between the two countries. In 2007, when my son was in his twenties, he traveled with me to the war zone of Darfur. When our children were young, my wife, Carolyn, and I took them both to Dachau, the first Nazi concentration camp, which opened in 1933 shortly after Adolf Hitler became chancellor of Germany. At Dachau, countless thousands of Jews and other prisoners were executed or died of malnutrition, disease, and overwork. We made a point of showing them the building where Christian prisoners were held after arrest for hiding Jews as part of a liberation movement. Now, as a grandparent, I hold myself accountable for making sure that my grandchildren also witness the risk and cost that may be required in following the rebel Jesus.

The Lenten season is the perfect time to reevaluate our lifestyle. During Lent, this season of introspection, we need to ask ourselves some challenging questions, both as individuals and as a church. Where have we accommodated our lives to worldly values instead of Kingdom values, to worldly politics instead of a new Kingdom community? What are we saying to our children? More importantly, what are we modeling to them? In what ways do we need to fast and to repent?

Challenging ourselves in this way is what the new birth in Jesus is all about. Being born again is like being transported from one kingdom, the kingdom of the world, to the kingdom of God. Yet we also have to give ourselves the same grace as Jesus extended to us. We are works in progress. At the time of our conversion, we basically say to Jesus, "I am all in, but I am not perfect." We must trust Jesus for our salvation, knowing that, left to our own devices and resources, we will never be good enough to have earned it. But our righteousness is not our own; our righteousness is in Christ and through what Jesus did for us in his death on the cross and resurrection. I have been walking with Jesus for more than forty years, and I am still in the process of detoxification from all that the world preaches and practices that does not reflect God's kingdom.

Mother Teresa once gave a pastor acquaintance of mine some of the best preaching advice I have ever heard. My friend was traveling through India and on a whim decided to visit the Missionaries of Charity headquarters, where he was surprised to meet the tiny yet indefatigable Mother Teresa in person. He asked her, "What advice might you have to offer a young preacher?" Her response: "Preach Jesus, the true Jesus, the real Jesus, the resurrected Jesus, and not a Jesus of people's imaginations."[6] As Christ followers, all of us this Lenten season must commit ourselves to realigning our lifestyles with the renegade gospel of the real and rebel Jesus. We must stop remaking Jesus into our own image.

If you are ready to make that commitment, pray this prayer with me:

Lord, in the midst of my doubt, skepticism, and uncertainty, I make the commitment today not only to confess you with my lips as Lord Jesus but to go where you are going and do what you are doing. I will leave no route for retreat or escape. I will be called by your name, and I will be numbered among your people. And it is in your name, Jesus, that I pray. Amen.

CHAPTER THREE

THE MOST IMPORTANT QUESTION
YOU WILL EVER HAVE TO ANSWER

Chapter Three
The Most Important Question You Will Ever Have to Answer

"But what about you?" he asked.
"Who do you say I am?"
(Luke 9:20)

A few years ago, Ginghamsburg's media producer drove into downtown Dayton, Ohio, to capture footage for an "on the street" video to use in worship. In recording the video, the producer asked a question of random people he encountered in a public space. The question the media producer asked was the most important question each of us will ever have to answer: "Who is Jesus?" Here is a sampling of the responses that day:

"Who is Jesus? Oh boy, a man that lived long ago and he gave his . . . umm, what is it he gave? He died for our sins."

"There are all kinds of fables out there. Some have been proven; some haven't."

"The son of God."

"Jesus was a good guy. He was trying to do good, but he was just an ordinary man."

"I don't believe that he is God. I don't think that he floats around like a ghost or something."

"Oh, I don't want to answer that question."

"He was a good teacher and a prophet."

"Oh, Lord!"

As you can see, the answers were wide-ranging, and the question seemed to make many responders uncomfortable.

Jesus himself asked this same question of his twelve disciples. They were by no means exempted from having to give an answer. Look at Luke 9:18-20 (CEB):

Once when Jesus was praying by himself, the disciples joined him, and he asked them, "Who do the crowds say that I am?" They answered, "John the Baptist, others Elijah, and still others that one of the ancient prophets has come back to life." He asked them, "And what about you? Who do you say that I am?" Peter answered, "The Christ sent from God."

When Jesus asked his disciples this crucial question, he had already been traveling with them, daily in their presence, for approximately 18 months. The title "rabbi" was used to describe Jesus multiple times in the New Testament. Being a rabbi in Jesus' time was a big deal. To Jewish boys, being accepted by a rabbi as his disciple represented the pinnacle of success. Jesus' disciples, many common men and laborers, must have been particularly surprised and delighted to have been chosen. Disciples followed their rabbis very closely, wanting to soak in every possible moment of learning and wisdom. As author Lois Tverberg has noted, disciples were urged to be "covered in the dust of your Rabbi." In other words, they were to follow their rabbi so closely that the dust kicked up by his feet as he walked along the road or path would coat their cloak and hair.[1]

Jesus was their rabbi, so where Jesus journeyed, the disciples journeyed. Where Jesus ate, the disciples ate. Wherever and whenever Jesus slept, they slept. Throughout these months with Jesus, the disciples had witnessed him performing miracles and had experienced his power working through them as they themselves performed extraordinary feats. Yet, the disciples were still accountable for making a decision about Jesus' identity.

JESUS AND HISTORY

No other single individual has had more impact on history than Jesus. More books have been written about Jesus than any other historical figure, and the Bible remains a perennial bestseller. To those who say Jesus was a myth, the calendar system itself refutes that claim. How we date time not only provides significant evidence of Jesus as a historical figure but also reveals how deeply the birth, death, and resurrection of Jesus have marked history. The term B.C. is an abbreviation for "Before Christ" and is used to denote years or time periods that occurred before Jesus' birth. A.D. represents "anno Domini," which is Latin for "in the year of our Lord," and denotes time periods that fall after Christ's birth. In academic circles the world has now secularized those terms, using CE (Common Era) or BCE (Before the Common Era) as replacements. Yet the use of B.C. and A.D. persists into the twenty-first century.

Multiple references to Jesus exist in other nonbiblical, historical records.

Many people have attempted to refute the historical Jesus' very existence by claiming you can't use the Bible to prove the Bible. In actuality, multiple references to Jesus exist in other nonbiblical, historical records. One key example is the first-century Jewish historian Josephus, who mentioned Jesus and Jesus' "cult-like" following in his historical work *Jewish Antiquities*.

Roman historian Tacitus referred to Jesus and to Emperor Nero's persecution of Christians in writings produced circa A.D. 115.[2] Pliny the Younger, a Roman governor, wrote the Roman emperor Trajan in A.D. 112, asking about how to conduct legal proceedings against Christians and noting that they sang hymns to Jesus "as to a god."[3] These historical voices were clearly all nonsympathetic, and yet within decades of his death they acknowledged Jesus as a historical person and also alluded to the early Christians' belief in Jesus' divinity.

Other religions' sacred writings also reference Jesus, including the Qur'an, which serves as the central religious text of Islam and is considered by Muslims to be a revelation from God. In my research I have been able to find at least twenty-five references to Jesus in the Qur'an that affirm his virgin birth, his miracles, and his healings. One notable mention is found in Qur'an 3:45-48:

When the angels said: O Mary, surely Allah gives thee good news with a word from Him (of one) whose name is the Messiah, Jesus, son of Mary, worthy of regard in this world and the Hereafter, and of those who are drawn nigh (to Allah), And he will speak to the people when in the cradle and when of old age, and (he will be) one of the good ones. She said: My Lord, how can I have a son and man has not yet touched me? He said: Even so; Allah creates what He pleases. When He decrees a matter, He only says to it, Be, and it is. And He will teach him the Book and the Wisdom and the Torah and the Gospel.[4]

Verse 49 goes on to state ". . . and I heal the blind and the leprous, and bring the dead to life with Allah's permission." Although Muslims don't believe Jesus to be divine, they revere him and consider him a great prophet. On one of my visits to Khartoum, Sudan, en route to visit Ginghamsburg's humanitarian projects in Darfur, I remember having a conversation with a Muslim friend in which he said, "You can't be a good Muslim if you don't believe in Jesus as one of Allah's prophets."

Great historical figures who did not believe in Jesus' divinity still attested to his existence as an extraordinary moral teacher. Mohandas Gandhi, the leader of the nonviolent civil disobedience movement that freed India from British rule, is one example. Born and raised a Hindu, Gandhi committed his life to living out the principles that Jesus taught in the Sermon on the Mount, found in Matthew 5–7. Gandhi once stated, "I like your Christ. I do not like your Christians. Your Christians are so unlike your Christ."

American founding father Thomas Jefferson was a Deist. Jefferson believed in the existence of a Supreme Being who was the creator and sustainer of the universe and the ultimate ground of being, but this was not the triune deity of orthodox Christianity. He also rejected the idea of Christ's divinity, but as he wrote to William Short on October 31, 1819, he was convinced that "the fragmentary teachings of Jesus constituted the outlines of a system of the most sublime morality which has ever fallen from the lips of man."[5] Jefferson created his own version of Scripture in which he removed all Jesus' miracles, claims of divinity, and resurrection, effectively reducing the Bible to a series of moral teachings. He never claimed that Jesus did not exist.

JESUS AND SKEPTICS

Skeptics abound, and Jesus' claim of divinity has remained controversial throughout the ages. More recently, the Jesus Seminar, a group of about 150 scholars formed in the late twentieth century, actively worked to discredit or eliminate from the Bible, much as Jefferson once did, any references to Jesus' miracles or other supernatural occurrences and acts. The Jesus Seminar described the Resurrection as symbolic, not literal. The seminar members would read Scripture and then vote with colored beads to determine a collective view of the historicity of Jesus' words and deeds. The seminar did not dispute Jesus as a historical figure, but they did not believe he was divine.

C. S. Lewis, author of some of my favorite books including *The Chronicles of Narnia*, was an atheist until his friend J. R. R. Tolkien, author of *Lord of the Rings*, led him to Jesus. Lewis was well aware of Jesus' claims of divinity. For example, in John 14:9, Jesus said, "Anyone who has seen me has seen the Father." In John 14:6-7, Jesus stated, "I am the way and the truth and the life. No one comes to the Father except through me. If you really know me, you will know my Father as well. From now on, you do know him and have seen him." These are bold claims, and Lewis knew it.

After his conversion to Christ, Lewis went on to write one of the classic Christian apologetics texts—*Mere Christianity*—in which he addressed the issue of Jesus' divinity in this way:

> A man who was merely a man and said the sort of things Jesus said would not be a great moral teacher. He would either be a lunatic—on a level with a man who says he is a poached egg—or else he would be the Devil of Hell. You must make your choice. Either this man was, and is, the Son of God; or else a madman or something worse."[6]

In other words, Lewis said we have only three choices. The first choice is that Jesus was a liar, which does not match the high moral integrity of Jesus' teachings or his way of life. When Jesus asked some of his religious detractors in John 8:46, "Can any of you prove me guilty of sin?" the question was met with silence.

A second choice is that Jesus was a lunatic. When I was working on my degree in social work at the University of Cincinnati, I served for a period of time in the psychiatric unit at the University of Cincinnati Medical Center. I met people who claimed to be God or Jesus, but their observable character was in no way consistent with the character demonstrated in Jesus' life.

The third and final choice is that Jesus was who he claimed to be: Lord. This argument for Christ's divinity came to be known as Lewis's trilemma. As Lewis put it, Jesus is a liar, lunatic, or Lord. He left little room for any other conclusion to be drawn.

C. S. Lewis was not the only atheist who, in the process of investigating Jesus' claims, became a Jesus follower. One of my contemporaries and a former atheist is Lee Strobel, who served as an investigative reporter for *The Chicago Tribune* as well as an attorney. I once had the honor of being interviewed by Strobel in a radio program that he hosted. Strobel, prompted by the positive changes he observed in his wife's life after her conversion experience with Jesus, set out on an intensive two-year investigation into the facts regarding Christianity. Through that process, he encountered Jesus for himself. I highly recommend *The Case for Christ*, the book Strobel penned that details the investigation and his findings.[7]

Some people use the apparent chasm between Christianity and science as the reason for not believing in a transcendent God, much less the divinity of Jesus. Yet Dr. Francis S. Collins, who served as the head of the Human Genome Project, elegantly argued in his book *The Language of God* that "belief in God can be an entirely rational choice and that the principles of faith are, in fact, complementary with the principles of science." Dr. Collins stated that the work of sequencing the human genome had been "both a stunning scientific achievement and an occasion of worship." Dr. Collins is both a respected scientist and a professing Christian who believes in the literal resurrection of Jesus Christ.[8] Let's return to the all-important question at the beginning of this chapter, found in Luke 9:20 (CEB):

> He asked them, "And what about you? Who do you say that I am?" Peter answered, "The Christ sent from God."

Does your response to the question match Peter's?

Now that we have explored the question from historical, skeptical, and scientific perspectives, let's take a personal look.

THE POWER OF MULTIPLICATION

It's been said that there are no atheists in foxholes, meaning that in times of crisis, people turn to God. The process of acquiring faith, however, is typically much more gradual and progressive. As I described earlier, my faith was developed over a two-year period. I first became a serious initiate and explorer of Jesus' teachings before I said to Jesus, "You are the Lord. You are the Christ sent from God. You are the alpha and omega, the first and the last, and I am your servant." Many times as a pastor I have been criticized for not making more use of the "altar call," a moment at the end of worship in which people are called forward to pray a simple prayer that will invite Jesus into their lives. Altar calls are not mentioned in the Bible but became popular in the late 1800s when they were deployed by the famous nineteenth-century revivalist Charles Finney, in part as a tool to sign converts up for the abolition movement.[9] To me, most altar calls represent easy believism—that is, they invite people to an acquaintance with an institutionalized Jesus, a Sunday school Jesus, and not the resurrected Lord of the universe. Faith is not that quick; faith is not that easy. Remember that Jesus did not pose the essential question of his identity to his disciples until they had been traveling with him, coated in his dust, for eighteen months.

Growing in faith is not just progressive in nature; it also happens best within the context of community. Look at Luke 9:1-2: "When Jesus had called the Twelve together, he gave them power and authority to drive out all demons and to cure diseases, and he sent them out to proclaim the kingdom of God and to heal the sick." Active faith in Jesus is not a solitary sport. It is difficult to discover the divinity of Jesus or the power of Jesus by yourself. Instead, Jesus is revealed in community.

When I was admitted to the University of Cincinnati at age eighteen, I was exploring Jesus but not yet fully committed to Jesus. I felt an odd sense that I was being pulled toward ministry, even though I didn't yet know that Jesus is Messiah, Jesus is God.

I became part of a small group of Christian friends, and though that was forty-five years ago, I still remember their names: Tony, Dwight, Ron, Mimi, Pam, Cathy. Through those friendships and our time of doing life together, I began to discover who Jesus is and to trust fully in Jesus' divinity. I also began to experience Jesus' power through connection into community. When the twelve disciples were called together, they were empowered to cure diseases and drive out demons in Jesus' name—nothing they ever would have attempted as solo acts. The power of Jesus works through us when we are together in a manner that does not happen when we are alone.

Mustard seed groups of students came together to be the power of light in the midst of darkness.

The power of community was apparent when I was a student during the tumultuous days of the Vietnam War protests in 1969 and 1970. In the spring of my freshman year, students took over the administration building on the University of Cincinnati campus, and the Ohio National Guard was deployed. The Kent State shooting happened nearby on May 4, 1970. As part of the Jesus Movement, though, mustard seed groups of students like my own came together to be the power of light in the midst of darkness. In contrast to the actions of militant protestors as well as those of state and federal officials, the Jesus Movement students became part of *ekklesia*, demonstrating the love of Christ and nonviolent means to seek justice and peace, both domestically and in Vietnam.

When we are part of a community and committed to it, we experience power that we don't possess when alone. In John 15:5, Jesus describes himself as the source of life, the vine that makes the branches possible. Note that "branches" is plural. When we as a community are intertwined with one another and connected to Jesus as Lord, we will "bear much fruit." Without Jesus, without that connectedness, we "can do nothing."

The power of community was also evidenced in Luke 9:10-17 in the feeding of the five thousand, just before Jesus posed the identity question to his disciples. By this point, Jesus had started attracting large crowds whenever he stopped and spoke. In this particular story, Jesus had stopped near Bethsaida and had drawn a crowd large enough to represent about five thousand households. As it became late afternoon, Jesus' disciples grew nervous about feeding such a large crowd. They encouraged Jesus to send the people away to get food and lodging for themselves and their families, but Jesus responded, "You give them something to eat" (Luke 9:13).

As God's son in the flesh, Jesus could simply have snapped his fingers and made food appear; but throughout the Gospels he chose to reveal his divinity through people gathered together in community. In doing so, Jesus showed that he can do more through our limitations within community than we can ever hope to accomplish using our own strength. We see our limitations; Christ reveals our possibilities.

I experienced this in my own life as an eighteen-year-old. I had copious excuses as to why Jesus would not be able to work through me. I graduated from my high school ranked 138th academically out of 152, including eight student below me who had dropped out. I felt like a disappointment to my parents. There were many "But, Lord" excuses on my resume. However, I learned that I didn't discover Jesus' divinity sitting in a chair by myself; I discovered it in community with others as I was willing to go out into the world, handing to Jesus my limited resources and abilities for Jesus to multiply.

When Jesus commanded the disciples to feed the people, the disciples responded that they had only five loaves of bread and two fish (Luke 9:13). That word *only* will limit us every time. Yet when the disciples released what they did have into Jesus' hands, Jesus blessed it, gave it back, and it was multiplied. The crowd was fed, and there were twelve baskets of leftovers.

I have witnessed many times the power of multiplication when we release what we have back into Jesus' hands for his purposes. Perhaps the most powerful time for me was in 2005, when the proceeds of Ginghamsburg's first annual Christmas Miracle Offering, which has since resulted in more than $7 million of humanitarian investment into Sudan and South Sudan, was used to initiate a sustainable agricultural program in Darfur. That first offering put 5,209 households back into the farming business and provided the income for families to buy back 900 of their children from indentured servanthood. I had a very vivid Jesus encounter upon learning this. I felt Jesus at my shoulder when I was visiting the project in Darfur as a firsthand witness to the miracle of multiplication. I couldn't see Jesus, but his presence was very real to me as he reminded me of this story of the feeding of the five thousand. He said, "Remember the feeding of the five thousand? It was really 5,209. We rounded it off for biblical purposes." Jesus promised in John 14:12, "Very truly I tell you, whoever believes in me will do the works I have been doing, and they will do even greater things than these, because I am going to the Father."

My experience of Jesus' divinity in 2005 wasn't because he snapped his fingers and conjured provision out of thin air. Instead, he invited the Ginghamsburg Church community to be a part of a multiplication miracle of biblical proportions when we faithfully pooled and released our resources into Jesus' hands. Time and again we witness Jesus' divinity within a community of followers as we remember to collectively release our assets, not sit on them. Note that in the Gospel of Matthew, it was only after Jesus had enabled his disciples to see the power of multiplication within community by feeding the five thousand (Chapter 14) that he asked his key question: "Who do you say I that am?" (Matthew 16:15 CEB).

A WHOLE LIFE COMMITMENT

Regardless of how we reach our response to Jesus' key question, much more is required than simply answering, "The Christ sent from God." Responding effectively to that question requires a whole life commitment. It means acknowledging and fully embracing what Jesus was as a man and who he is as divine God. Jesus is the best picture I could ever imagine of a God I want to follow. In human form, Jesus demonstrated that God is not an unconcerned, disembodied entity who is emotionally detached from our pain and suffering, but rather a God who chooses to enter into that suffering with us. Jesus gives flesh and reality to a God who cares, loves us deeply, and longs to win us at all costs, even to the point of death on the cross. Perhaps it was expressed best by author and Christian humanist Dorothy Sayers:

> For whatever reason God chose to make man as he is—limited and suffering and subject to sorrows and death—he had the honesty and courage to take his own medicine.... He has himself gone through the whole of human experience, from the trivial irritations of family life and the cramping restrictions of hard work and lack of money to the worst horrors of pain and humiliation, defeat, despair and death. When he was a man, he played the man. He was born in poverty and died in disgrace and thought it well worthwhile.[10]

The parables that Jesus shared with his disciples in Luke 15 further reveal God's heart. Jesus first described God as a shepherd who spends hours combing the countryside for one lost sheep while ninety-nine others are safely pastured at home—a shepherd who then excitedly throws a party to celebrate once the lone lost sheep is found. Then God is a woman who has lost a coin and will not rest, laboring and searching unceasingly until the lost has been retrieved; once again, there's a party. Finally Jesus told perhaps the greatest parable of all: a father welcomes with open arms a foolish and lost son (often called the prodigal son or wayward son); then, once again, throws a party. You have to love a God who is always throwing a party in honor of someone who has done nothing to merit it. Hearing those parables, I can believe in a God who looks and sounds like Jesus.

Eyewitnesses from the New Testament community clearly understood the physical resurrection of Jesus Christ and embraced his identity as Messiah—as fully divine. (In Chapter Six, we will examine the implications of Jesus' resurrection much more carefully.) The Apostle Paul penned this hymn about Christ in his letter to the Colossians during A.D. 62, just over thirty years after Jesus' resurrection.

> The Son is the image of the invisible God, the firstborn over all creation. For in him all things were created: things in heaven and on earth, visible and invisible, whether thrones or powers or rulers or authorities; all things have been created through him and for him. He is before all things, and in him all things hold together. And he is the head of the body, the church; he is the beginning and the firstborn from among the dead, so that in everything he might have the supremacy.
> (Colossians 1:15-18)

In essence, Paul's declaration emphasized that Christ is the divine mind making all of creation's systems work, whether the gravity that tethers us to earth, the mixture of oxygen and nitrogen that sustains our breath, the earth's precise distance from the sun so that the planet can support life, or the involuntary muscles ensuring that my heart beats and my lungs breathe. Verse 18 reminds us that in everything, Christ has supremacy. The last time I checked, *everything* in the Greek means "everything"—my life priorities, my time, my wants, my money, my family, my career. In everything I choose to do, Jesus Christ has supremacy.

Right after Jesus asked the key question "Who do you say that I am?" and Peter responded, "The Christ sent from God," Jesus shared in Luke 9:23-24 what could only have been a difficult concept to embrace for his disciples, the rabbi's most enthusiastic followers: "'All who want to come after me must say no to themselves, take up their cross daily, and follow me. All who want to save their lives will lose them. But all who lose their lives because of me will save them'" (CEB). The operative word is *daily*. A disciple must die to self and rise to new life in Christ each day after accepting Jesus Chris as Lord and Savior.

Note also that Jesus repeated his first and most persistent call to his disciples in verse 23: "Follow me." *Follow* is a verb; *following* means we cannot remain stationary. When I confess that Jesus Christ is the Messiah, the Son of God, I commit to follow Jesus in a lifestyle of sacrificial service, walking in the dust of my Rabbi. Whatever my Rabbi values, I value. Whatever my Rabbi thinks about God, I think about God. Whatever my Rabbi thinks about people, I think about people. Whatever my Rabbi believes about wealth, I believe about wealth. Whatever my Rabbi believes about the poor, I believe about the poor. Whatever my Rabbi believes about creation, I believe about creation. I act like my Rabbi, talk like my Rabbi, love like my Rabbi, and give my life away for my Rabbi's mission.

Unfortunately, many of us start that journey with enthusiasm but fail to sustain it. Our faith goes on cruise control as we start seeking comfort and not a calling. It doesn't help that too often in our churches we pigeonhole Jesus safely behind the altar rails and communion tables of our tame religious traditions, teaching people to revere Jesus instead of following Jesus sacrificially every day in the trenches of life. Jesus' call is not to revere; his call is to follow. When we do so, reverence will naturally result.

A Sunday Morning Habit

We struggle to follow Jesus, in part because our contemporary culture is saturated in a secular worldview. In this worldview, we operate as if God were not a factor. Jesus becomes a Sunday morning habit, and the rest of the week we seem to get along just fine without him. A secular worldview is also a materialistic worldview. We draw our security from our money and material possessions rather than from the promises of God.

Within our soft-secular churches, we claim to believe in God and profess Jesus but then act on the values of the secular culture. This explains why we struggle with the sacrifice required in following Jesus. Tithing is one example. Ginghamsburg Church is a healthy church in terms of stewardship and generous giving, and yet even here we have hundreds of families in the church who give nothing. Christians have brought Jesus into a secular worldview instead of bringing the secular world into Jesus' worldview.

If we are going to follow Jesus, recognizing Jesus as Messiah, we will have to radically realign our life priorities. Jesus brilliantly illustrated this in a parable found in Luke 14:16-24. Jesus described a man, representing God, who is hosting a large dinner and sends out his servants to invite guests to the party. One by one the excuses come back from the invited guests. One invitee indicates that he has just bought a farm and needs to examine his new land. A second has bought five teams of oxen and feels compelled to see if they are working out as planned. A third invitee claims that he has just gotten married and is still on his honeymoon. Notice that the three invitees use the same excuses we give when we choose to revere Jesus instead of following him: our material property, our work, and our relationships. These convenient excuses betray our real allegiances and show that we relegate Jesus to someone we worship at church one morning a week. We have reduced the true worship of Jesus to singing three praise and worship songs on Sunday mornings. In the Bible, God's people sang songs in front of Israel's armies as they marched off to war, not when sitting in religious meetings. What happened to the practice of following Jesus sacrificially?

One thing I know: each of us in our lifetime will answer Jesus' question, "Who do you say that I am?" Let's not deceive ourselves—not answering, ignoring, avoiding, belittling, or postponing the question is still a response. I have been traveling in the dust of my Rabbi for forty-five years and have never been completely free of doubt. In many ways, at the age of sixty-three I am still figuring this Jesus journey out. Yet despite periodic fear, failure, and setbacks, I can proclaim, like Peter, that the rebel Jesus is the Christ sent from God. Jesus has repeatedly revealed himself to me as Messiah and Lord when I have responded in faith to his call, witnessing the miracle of multiplication through the community of God's people as we place our resources, gifts, and lives into his hands.

Who is Jesus? One of the church's most ancient creeds, the Apostle's' Creed, proclaims the foundation on which I have staked my reputation, ministry, and life:

I believe in God, the Father Almighty,
    maker of heaven and earth;

And in Jesus Christ his only Son our Lord:
    who was conceived by the Holy Spirit,
        born of the Virgin Mary,
        suffered under Pontius Pilate,
        was crucified, dead, and buried;*
    the third day he rose from the dead;
    he ascended into heaven,
        and sitteth at the right hand of God the
        Father Almighty;
    from thence he shall come to judge the quick
    and the dead.

I believe in the Holy Spirit,
    the holy catholic** church,
    the communion of saints,
    the forgiveness of sins,
    the resurrection of the body,
    and the life everlasting. Amen.[11]

---

*Traditional use of this creed includes these words: "He descended into hell."
***universal*

CHAPTER FOUR
SEEING JESUS TODAY

CHAPTER FOUR
SEEING JESUS TODAY

"Sir," they said, "we would like to see Jesus."
(John 12:21)

Each morning I am in my study early spending time in God's word and in prayer. I know that if I don't make daily devotion with God the first priority of my day, then within less than twenty-four hours I risk losing a healthy fear of God. Without Jesus, I am aware how easily I could become a complete jerk. So, I enjoy my time spent in the Gospels of Matthew, Mark, Luke, and John reading about Jesus, his miracles, his teachings, and his relationships. I can think about the historical Jesus and reminisce about my own early encounters with Jesus during the Jesus Movement. However, if I am not careful I can easily fall into the trap of the "same old, same old," soon basing my entire relationship with Jesus on rereading the same two-thousand-year-old stories or reminiscing how I experienced

Jesus in the past. If I limit myself to reading the old stories, hearing the same sermons, and reliving past moments, I fail to seek the real and present Jesus of the here and now.

THE POWER OF EXPECTATION

In Matthew 25:1-13, Jesus told a parable of ten virgins who are standing with their lamps outside at night awaiting the arrival of a wedding procession. In biblical times, that procession traditionally would travel from the bride's home to the new husband's. In the parable, Christ is the awaited bridegroom. Jesus noted that five of the women were foolish and five wise. The foolish women had their lamps but had failed to bring oil for them. The wise women were fully stocked with both. Because the groom's arrival was delayed, the waiting women became drowsy and fell asleep. We can read this as an indictment of today's church, which also has become drowsy and has fallen asleep awaiting Christ's return. Jesus continued the parable in verses 6 to 12:

> "At midnight the cry rang out: 'Here's the bridegroom! Come out to meet him!'

> "Then all the virgins woke up and trimmed their lamps. The foolish ones said to the wise, 'Give us some of your oil; our lamps are going out.'

> " 'No,' they replied, 'there may not be enough for both us and you. Instead, go to those who sell oil and buy some for yourselves.'

> "But while they were on their way to buy the oil, the bridegroom arrived. The virgins who were ready went

in with him to the wedding banquet. And the door was shut.

"Later the others also came. 'Lord, Lord,' they said, 'open the door for us!'

"But he replied, 'Truly I tell you, I don't know you.'"

This parable of the bridesmaids is about the power of expectation. If we want to see the bridegroom, if we want to see and experience Jesus today, we need to seek him expectantly and actively. The bottom line is that you will find Jesus only if you are looking for him.

When my children were small, my wife, Carolyn, and I would load them into the car on spring breaks and drive to Florida. Tipp City, Ohio, where we lived, was approximately sixty to ninety minutes north of Cincinnati, depending on traffic. We would barely get across the bridge into Kentucky when the kids would start asking the most famous and most repeated question children ever ask on vacation: "Are we there yet?" I would tell them, "No! We still have eighteen hours to go."

To pass the time, Carolyn and I would use a variety of car games as a distraction. For instance, I would tell Kristen and Jonathan that the first person who spotted a Canadian license plate would win ten thousand points. (As any experienced parent knows, there always have to be points involved.) Inevitably, the next question would be, "What are the points for, Dad?" I would promise that the points could be cashed in for ice cream or something else inexpensive yet sure to appeal to a kid's heart (or sweet tooth). Canadian license plates seemed like a safe bet to keep the children busy for a while, since it's a different country. However, it was amazing how quickly either Kristen or Jonathan would rake in those points. Having failed to keep them busy the first time, I would choose what seemed to be a difficult state from the West, such as Montana. Once again, in no time I would be forking over points. By the time we reached Tennessee, the math became exceedingly difficult to track. The truth is, on Interstate 75 we are often surrounded by license plates from Canada and Montana, but we don't see them because we are not looking for them. The power of expectation means that you find what you are looking for.

Periodically I lead trips of Ginghamsburg members to Israel. One of the sites we visit is Tel Megiddo, a place of historical significance since it guarded a narrow pass and trade route connecting Assyria and Egypt and was the site of several ancient battles. Megiddo was inhabited from approximately 7000 to 586 B.C. As church members trample around looking at the ruins, they pay scant attention to the dusty rocks at their feet. In truth, some of those "rocks" are actually shards of ancient pottery. On my first two visits to Megiddo, I also had not paid much attention to the ground beneath me—until on my third trip, one of my travel companions was an archaeologist. He helped train my eye to look for the shards and showed me how to tell which fragments may have dated back to the days of Abraham, approximately three thousand years before; which were Hebrew; and which were Philistine. He taught me that the potter's wheel was invented in roughly 3000 B.C., so fragments that showed evidence of a potter's wheel were more recent, and pottery made without a wheel may have dated back to the days of Abraham. For more recent pottery there was another test: Hebrews did not decorate their pottery because decorations implied a lack of humility, while Philistines painted their pottery. Now when I am in Megiddo, the shards are all that I see—the power of expectation.

This power of expectation is why Jesus said in Matthew 7:7-8: "'Ask and it will be given to you; seek and you will find; knock and the door will be opened to you. For everyone who asks receives; the one who seeks finds; and to the one who knocks, the door will be opened.'"

It's important to note that in the original Greek, the verbs used in that passage are in present continuous tense—that is, a more accurate reading of the verbs might be, "Ask and keep on asking. ... Seek and keep on seeking. ..." Expectation needs to be constant and ongoing—a daily, intentional, whole-life priority of seeking the presence of Christ today, of actively listening for Christ's voice in the present.

Now that Jesus' physical presence is removed, the world can no longer see him, but we can.

In John 14:15-17, Jesus made a promise about experiencing Jesus in the here and now: "'If you love me, keep my commands. And I will ask the Father, and he will give you another advocate to help you and be with you forever—the Spirit of truth.'" The Bible, to which I dedicate the first moments of my day, is the most important book in the world; but note that when Jesus left he didn't say he would leave us with a book, but with his presence in the form of the Holy Spirit. In verse 17 Jesus went on: "'The world cannot accept him, because it neither sees him nor knows him. But you know him, for he lives with you and will be in you.'" Jesus knew that we would need fresh information and inspiration, not just the ancient stories about what he told the woman at the well, how he healed the leper, or how he called Zacchaeus out of the tree. Jesus continued in verses 18-19: "'I will not leave you as orphans; I will come to you. Before long, the world will not see me anymore, but you will see me. Because I live, you also will live.'"

When Jesus walked Planet Earth, everyone could see him in the flesh—friends, followers, and foes. We no longer have that opportunity. Now that Jesus' physical presence is removed, the world can no longer see him, but we can. Those who are born of the Spirit are able to experience and see him today. When we ask, seek, and knock in expectation, we find what we are looking for.

INVESTING OUR GIFTS

We opened this chapter with the parable of the bridesmaids, told by Jesus in Matthew 25:1-13. A second parable is told in verses 14-30. Often referred to as the parable of the talents, it tells the story of a wealthy man who is about to leave on a journey. The man calls over three servants and explains that he is entrusting his wealth to them while he is away. Jesus is the wealthy man in the parable, who has entrusted his wealth to us in the form of our gifts, talents, and treasures. In the story, our limitations are contrasted with Christ's limitlessness. We learn that the first servant invested his five bags of gold and gained five more bags of gold. The second servant took his two bags, put the investment to work, and doubled it. The final servant, fearful and timid, hid his one bag of gold and gained nothing, which merited the master's wrath upon his return.

Like the servants in the parable, we are not to hoard our gifts from God but invest them for Christ's miracle of multiplication. My book *Dare to Dream* is designed to help people begin to invest in this way by discovering their life missions. It is in the execution of our life missions that we see Jesus today. Each of us has a BHAG—a big hairy audacious God-purpose—which in many cases is different from our day job. Bono from the band U2, for example, has a day job in music; but his BHAG is to eradicate severe poverty, especially in Africa.

During my senior year in high school I was part of a rock band. We called ourselves Lyme Street Station and ran a teen club called the Lost Dimension. Looking back, I can see how appropriate the club name was in describing my spirit and soul. One weekend I remember playing a gig with the band, hanging out with my girlfriend, and partying—a weekend which, in retrospect, I'm not particularly proud of. The following Monday I was walking outside the school with my girlfriend, and as we turned the corner we passed a large tree. At that moment, I clearly heard God speak to me. It wasn't an audible voice, and yet I clearly knew who it was. I did not have a relationship with Jesus. I was not thinking about God, much less was I concerned about being obedient to God. Yet I heard God in a still, silent, inner whisper. I turned to my girlfriend and said, "God just told me I am supposed to be a minister." You can imagine the look she gave me. Since that time, God has continued to turn my life upside down, especially when I start to become too comfortable or complacent. Be prepared. When you get serious about Jesus Christ and your life mission, he will completely mess up your life along with any preconceived notions you may have about how things are supposed to be. But, in this very disruption, it is also how you meet, experience, and follow Jesus in the world today.

My BHAG has taken me along with others into Vietnam to preach the word, even though I risked arrest for propagating religion. It has taken me into the war zone of Darfur, Sudan, three times, once accompanied by my son. It has caused me to spend thirty-five years in a job that requires nights and weekends. When I became serious about Jesus, it messed up my life. And I wouldn't have it any other way.

One reason so few of us encounter the living Jesus is that we have created a childlike storybook image of Jesus. We have made our faith pragmatic instead of revolutionary. An article in

The Christian Century put it this way: "In order to be politically or culturally acceptable, we've often stripped Christianity of Jesus or transformed him into a character he is not. We've made Jesus wimpy rather than revolutionary; tolerant rather than loving; good rather than God."[1] Jesus understood his own big hairy audacious God-purpose. The night of his arrest before being crucified, he prayed, "Now my soul is troubled, and what shall I say? 'Father, save me from this hour'?" Jesus then answered his own question: "No, it was for this very reason I came to this hour" (John 12:27). Jesus had to die to self, to both self-comfort and self-safety. And so do we. As we die to self, our lives become fertilizer to feed the seeds of Kingdom growth. We experience Jesus as we expectantly seek to find Jesus and as we follow through on that to which Jesus has called us.

Where Do We Find Jesus Today?

In the previous chapter we explored the first key question, "Who do you say that I am?" The next key question might be, "When do we see Jesus?" Let's turn to the parable of the sheep and goats in Matthew 25: "When the Son of Man comes in his glory, and all the angels with him, he will sit on his glorious throne. All the nations will be gathered before him, and he will separate the people one from another as a shepherd separates the sheep from the goats. He will put the sheep on his right and the goats on his left" (verses 31-33).

This parable illustrates what will happen on the Day of Judgment. I sometimes refer to it as my "final exam" Scripture. In telling the story, Jesus let us know what will be important when we stand face-to-face with God. What Jesus emphasized in the parable was not what the church tends to emphasize—that is, accepting Jesus and repenting of our sins. Those things are important, of course, but something else is given top billing:

"Then the King will say to those on his right, 'Come, you who are blessed by my Father; take your inheritance, the kingdom prepared for you since the creation of the world. For I was hungry and you gave me something to eat, I was thirsty and you gave me something to drink, I was a stranger and you invited me in, I needed clothes and you clothed me, I was sick and you looked after me, I was in prison and you came to visit me.'" (verses 34-36)

In the next verse, we find the operative word: see. "Then the righteous will answer him, 'Lord, when did we see you hungry and feed you, or thirsty and give you something to drink? When did we see you a stranger and invite you in, or needing clothes and clothe you? When did we see you sick or in prison and go to visit you?' (verses 37-39). The King's response is revealing: "Truly I tell you, whatever you did for one of the least of these brothers and sisters of mine, you did for me" (verse 40).

Where do we find Jesus today? He is not an otherworldly being to be sought out among the clouds. He has more to say about life, about us, and about our mission than what we can read in the Bible each day. We don't have to retreat to a monastery or temple to find him. The world is his temple; we are his temple. We experience Jesus when we live out his mission and listen attentively and expectantly to the voice of the Holy Spirit, the companion that Jesus promised will guide us into all truth and tell us what is to come (John 16:13).

Usually when God speaks, it is not as dramatic as my experience outside the high school when I was eighteen. God often uses more normal means. For instance, the seeds of Ginghamsburg's involvement in humanitarian projects in Sudan were planted when I kicked off my shoes one Sunday afternoon after preaching and started checking out an ad in the newspaper about a luxury sedan available for lease. However, I couldn't help but notice that across the page was a photo of a starving child in Sudan. Those juxtaposed images of the sedan and Sudan seared my heart and my conscience. If Jesus is Lord, why were sedans more important to me than Sudans?

More recently, God grabbed my attention about another area of need in the world that is breaking his heart—the deadly, persistent disease of malaria. Having said that, I must add that my involvement wasn't immediate. In 2008, The United Methodist Church started a program called "Imagine No Malaria" and pledged to raise $75 million to combat this preventable but killer disease. Because Ginghamsburg is one of the larger churches in the denomination, United Methodist leaders began to ask us to be a part. One of the United Methodist bishops approached me a few years ago asking for our involvement, especially since the disease takes the most lives in Africa, a continent particularly near to my heart. Although I was certainly sympathetic to this very worthwhile cause, I considered it important to continue our focus on our current local and Sudan initiatives. I responded to the bishop, thanking her for the invitation but indicating that we were already building schools, putting in water yards, and establishing clinics. There didn't seem to be room to add the fight against malaria as well. I tucked the idea away.

About a year later, my own West Ohio Conference received a new bishop who also had a significant passion for Imagine No Malaria and had raised funds at his previous post. The United Methodist General Board of Church and Society planned a "Day on the Hill" in Washington, DC in December 2012 for United Methodists to lobby Congress for malaria funding, and the bishop asked our church's executive director to go in the hopes of capturing our interest. Our executive director went and found the opportunity enlightening and the need urgent. However, I felt as a church we needed to stay our missional course.

Then one Saturday night the following April, I went home, brain-dead after preaching two messages to our Saturday night congregations, to share a bowl of popcorn with my wife and catch the night's featured film on HBO. The movie turned out to be HBO's premier of *Mary and Martha,* starring Hillary Swank and Brenda Blethyn, a movie about two mothers who became impassioned advocates for malaria research and prevention after each lost a son to the disease in Africa.[2] As I sat through parts of the movie with tears welling up in my eyes, I knew I had finally seen and heard Jesus. Later that month, the Ginghamsburg Leadership Board voted to raise $1 million over the next five years, in addition to our annual Miracle Offering, for Imagine No Malaria.

We all think we want to see God, but the Divine often shows up in places we least expect.

How do we experience Jesus today? Where do we see him? According to Jesus himself, "Truly I tell you, whatever you did for one of the least of these brothers and sisters of mine, you did for me" (Matthew 25:40). We all think we want to see God, but the Divine often shows up in places we least expect. We will see Jesus when, with an expectant heart, we take a walk on the sacrificial side and discover him in the everyday occurrences of life.

MISSING JESUS

I think there are a number of reasons why we so often fail to see Jesus in the life around us. Sometimes it's because we have faulty expectations. Since the invention of iTunes, my music collection has become largely digital. However, I do still have a collection of

CDs that I dust off periodically. Recently I was browsing my stack, looking for a specific CD that I had pictured in my mind as having a red cover. I couldn't find it. Becoming increasingly frustrated (I really wanted to hear that CD), I ran my finger along the spines of the collection two more times. No luck. Finally, I called to Carolyn asking if she knew what might have happened to it. Within seconds she walked over, pulled the right CD out of the stack I had been checking, and placed it in my hand. The cover was blue. I couldn't find the blue CD because I had been seeking a red one. When we have not been seeking the living and active Jesus, if we have tucked him away to be dusted off periodically only when the mood strikes us, we risk looking for the Sunday school Jesus of our childhood, a Jesus of our imagination, not a living Savior and Lord who is among us today.

We may also fail to see Jesus because of our lack of faith or our faith restrictions. There are miracles all around us, but we do not see them because of our bias or skepticism. My grandparents lived well into their nineties. In my seminary days, Carolyn and I frequently traveled between the seminary near Lexington, Kentucky, north into our hometown of Cincinnati where our parents lived. Often on that trip we would stop to visit my grandparents in their small house in northern Kentucky. I can still picture the house in my mind's eye—the recliner my grandfather occupied, along with the smaller chair that was grandmother's customary seat. Carolyn and I would be invited into the living room to sit on a couch that my grandmother always called a davenport. One visit stands out in particular. When I asked, "Grandmother, how are you doing?" the reply was, "Well, we're doing pretty good—as well as anyone could do at ninety-five, I guess. It's just that I've been having trouble with my eyes." When I asked about the eye trouble, she said, "It's like everything is blurry." I courteously pointed out that she was ninety-five and that "this kind of thing happens." She said,

"Yes, but this has all happened within the last two weeks." As I sat there, I then glanced over to my grandfather and it struck me. My grandmother was wearing my grandfather's glasses, and my grandfather was wearing my grandmother's. Your field of vision is bound to be restricted if you are wearing the wrong glasses.

From a time shortly after our birth, definitely by the time we have entered kindergarten, we have been given glasses that cause us to view the world around us through a secular lens. We are immersed in a culture of skepticism that teaches us there is a sharp division between fact and faith, that which is real and that which is religion. A secular worldview equates everything supernatural with superstition and always seeks some sort of "rational" explanation. As Jesus followers, we must refocus ourselves on viewing the world through the reality of Jesus and a Kingdom worldview. Ultimately the proclaimed "rationality" of a secular worldview is also a religion; it simply requires a different kind of faith. Ultimately, the religion of rationality is not necessarily rational, as it makes broad assumptions and jumps to unprovable conclusions.

In a conversation with the disciples described in Matthew 13, Jesus gave another reason why we do not see him or experience miracles. Jesus had just shared the parable of the sower with a large crowd, in which he pointed out the reasons why the good news of the gospel was not received or retained by many who listened. When the disciples asked Jesus why he taught in parables, Jesus responded:

"This is why I speak to them in parables:

'Though seeing, they do not see;
though hearing, they do not hear or understand.

In them is fulfilled the prophecy of Isaiah:

> "You will be ever hearing but never understanding;
>> you will be ever seeing but never perceiving.
> For this people's heart has become calloused;
>> they hardly hear with their ears,
>> and they have closed their eyes.
> Otherwise they might see with their eyes,
>> hear with their ears,
>> understand with their hearts
> and turn, and I would heal them.'"

(Matthew 13:13-15)

Sometimes the reason we do not see Jesus isn't our skepticism or intellectual doubt; it is because of our hardness of heart. When we cease to have our hearts broken by those tragedies, circumstances, and sufferings that break God's heart, when we fail to live more simply so that others may simply live, we are out of alignment with Christ, no longer in right relationship. We need to return to living and giving like God with skin on—Jesus.

Even though it's over a decade old, I still love the movie *Bruce Almighty*, starring Jim Carrey as down-on-his-luck news reporter Bruce Nolan and Morgan Freeman as God. When reporter Bruce is overlooked by his television station employer for a news anchor position that Bruce is convinced he deserved, he vehemently blames God for his misfortune. Morgan Freeman as God decides to do something about it and bequeaths the role of God to Bruce, humorously suggesting that perhaps Bruce will do a better job at it. Of course, after enjoying his new powers for a few days and improving his own life, Bruce begins to discover that the job is not nearly as easy or fulfilling as he had anticipated. Frustrated, Bruce consults with Morgan Freeman about how to make the whole thing work.

God tells him, "Parting your soup is not a miracle, Bruce. It's a magic trick. A single mom who's working two jobs and still finds time to take her kid to soccer practice, that's a miracle. A teenager who says 'no' to drugs and 'yes' to an education, that's a miracle. People want me to do everything for them. But what they don't realize is 'they' have the power. You want to see a miracle, son? Be the miracle."

Bruce protests, "What if I need you? What if I have questions?"

God smiles and answers, "That's your problem, Bruce. That's everybody's problem. You keep looking up."[3]

God's lines strike me each time I watch the movie. If we want to see a miracle, we need to **be** the miracle. Bruce's problem—the problem we all have—is that we keep looking up. We are trying to find Jesus in the extraordinary instead of the ordinary. That is why we miss him.

SPIRITUAL DROWSINESS

I was preparing my Palm Sunday sermon while writing this book, and I turned to the Luke 22 account of Jesus praying in the garden of Gethsemane on the night of his arrest. Jesus had just shared the final Passover meal with his disciples, their numbers dropping from twelve to eleven as Judas scurried out of the room to betray him. Not wanting to be alone on this bleakest of nights, Jesus brought his disciples with him as he retreated to the garden for prayer.

> On reaching the place, he said to them, "Pray that you will not fall into temptation." He withdrew about a stone's throw beyond them, knelt down and prayed, "Father, if you are willing, take this cup from me; yet not my will, but yours be done." An angel from heaven

appeared to him and strengthened him. And being in anguish, he prayed more earnestly, and his sweat was like drops of blood falling to the ground.

When he rose from prayer and went back to the disciples, he found them asleep, exhausted from sorrow. "Why are you sleeping?" he asked them. "Get up and pray so that you will not fall into temptation."

(Luke 22:40-46)

As I reread this familiar passage during Lent, Jesus' question to his disciples struck me as particularly significant: "Why are you sleeping?" As I thought about the lukewarm love and halfhearted commitment that many of us demonstrate toward the rebel Jesus today, I realized that this question reveals yet another significant reason why we don't recognize Jesus. We have fallen asleep and are no longer attentive to the Spirit's voice.

Sleepiness, even in the natural world, can be a significant problem. In a December 2013 article entitled "5 Other Disastrous Accidents Related to Sleep Deprivation," *The Huffington Post* reviewed just a few of the many accidents attributed at least in part to sleepiness that have resulted in loss of life as well as material damage.[4] The Chernobyl nuclear power plant explosion was one example. The engineers working that night had been on duty for thirteen hours or more at the time of the explosion. Likewise, the Three Mile Island nuclear incident in 1979 was "attributed to human error due to sleep deprivation." A few NASA managers supporting the disastrous Challenger space shuttle launch in 1986 had only two hours of sleep before reporting for duty. The Exxon Valdez oil spill in 1989 and American Airlines Flight 1420 crash in 1999 also had crew members working at far less than their best capacity and skill level because of sleep deprivation.

Short-term risks of sleep deprivation include decreased performance and alertness, memory impairment, and stress, as well as occupational and automobile accidents. Long-term health risks include high blood pressure, heart failure, stroke, and even obesity. Sleepiness is a serious issue![5]

Likewise, spiritual drowsiness is dangerous to our long-term health and well-being, not to mention to the efficacy and fruitfulness of the church. When we first encounter or recognize the rebel Jesus, for many of us there is a kind of adrenaline rush. We are all things Jesus all the time. But as that first love and passion fade, we become spiritually drowsy and are no longer able to see clearly the Christ to whom we committed our lives.

Do you find yourself nodding off spiritually? A warning sign for me is when I start to become easily distracted in my prayer life, or when I find myself idly Googling last night's baseball scores during my study time instead of listening for the Spirit. Do you ever open the Bible and find yourself returning repeatedly to the starting point because you stopped paying attention a few verses in? Do you read popular bestsellers about the Bible instead of the Bible itself? Have you slipped into the habit of watching worship online instead of joining the body of believers in person? Have you defaulted to your computer or television screen as you "church" instead of as a convenient alternative for when you are ill, traveling, or snowed in?

In Matthew's account of Jesus praying in the garden of Gethsemane, Jesus said to the disciples, "My soul is overwhelmed with sorrow to the point of death. Stay here and keep watch with me" (Matthew 26:38). When Jesus returned later to find them sleeping he implored, "Couldn't you men keep watch with me for one hour?" and he warned them to "watch and pray so that you will not fall into temptation" (verses 40-41). Jesus' use of the word *watch* evokes the image of a guard looking out over an ancient city, assigned to stay alert and vigilant while the rest of the community sleeps, ensuring the well-being of all within the city's walls.

To see Christ today, we need to wake up, stay alert, and stop wallowing in complacency, comfort, and spiritual sleep. We need to remain connected to a community of fellow Jesus followers who will hold us accountable. Most of all, we need constantly to be aware of our dependence on God. Jesus himself modeled this. Going back to Luke's account, we read, "Jesus went out as usual to the Mount of Olives, and his disciples followed him" (Luke 22:39). In other words, prayer on the Mount of Olives was not an extraordinary, one-time event for Jesus during a moment of intense crisis; it was his habit to do so.

We can live in a vital relationship with the rebel Jesus today. We do not have to rely simply on the written word or ancient stories to sustain our faith and battle our doubts when the living Word is accessible right in this moment. It begins with the power of expectation. We will find what we actively seek and hear that for which we earnestly listen. It culminates in our life mission as servants and coworkers with a living and active Christ.

As we close this chapter, my prayer for you is the same as the one the Apostle Paul prayed for the believers in Ephesus:

> I pray that the God of our Lord Jesus Christ, the Father of glory, will give you a spirit of wisdom and revelation that makes God known to you. I pray that the eyes of your heart will have enough light to see what is the hope of God's call, what is the richness of God's glorious inheritance among believers, and what is the overwhelming greatness of God's power that is working among us believers. (Ephesians 1:17-19 CEB)

CHAPTER FIVE
THE WAY OF THE CROSS

CHAPTER FIVE
THE WAY OF THE CROSS

Whoever wants to be my disciple must deny themselves
and take up their cross daily and follow me.
(Luke 9:23)

Jesus' journey to the cross began several months before his fateful ride into the Holy City on that day we now refer to as Palm Sunday. Luke tells us in his Gospel, "As the time approached for him to be taken up to heaven, Jesus resolutely set out for Jerusalem" (Luke 9:51).

Shortly before his last pilgrimage to Jerusalem began, however, Jesus asked the disciples two questions that led them, and ultimately will lead us, to answer yes or no to following the way of the cross. His first question was "Who do the crowds say I am?" The disciples answered the way a seminary student might: "Some say John the Baptist; others say Elijah; and still others, that one of of the prophets of long ago has come back to life" (Luke 9:18-19). But Jesus wanted a personal answer, not a theological one. So he asked the second question, the question we explored in Chapter Three that each of us must answer: "Who do you say that I am?" Peter then made the declaration that would eventually determine his own fate: "The Christ sent from God" (verse 20 CEB).

Immediately following Peter's declaration, Jesus made known his own impending rejection, suffering, death, and resurrection. Then he issued the hard challenge that is laid down for anyone who accepts Jesus' invitation to become a follower: "Whoever wants to be my disciple must deny themselves and take up their cross daily and follow me. For whoever wants to save their life will lose it, but whoever loses their life for me will save it. What good is it for someone to gain the whole world, and yet lose or forfeit their very self?" (verses 23-25). As the disciples learned, Jesus does not allow us to reduce discipleship to a theoretical belief system or a construct of orthodox doctrines. To make the declaration "Jesus is Lord" means an all-in, whole-life commitment to follow Jesus in an alternative, sacrificial way of life, fully pledging one's allegiance to the rebel Jesus in faithfully serving the renegade gospel.

The Cost of Following Christ

The Lenten season (forty days leading up to Easter excluding Sundays) begins on Ash Wednesday. For Christians, Lent marks an intentional time of self-reflection and repentance. It is a time to lay distractions aside, to move beyond tepid faith and the accommodations made to self-focused secular values. Christians choose to fast, or lay aside, daily activities or habits practiced most of the year so that we may be more fully focused and engaged in following Jesus in authentic discipleship.

Jesus' final trip to Jerusalem leading up to his arrest and crucifixion gives crystal clarity to the meaning of the cross and the cost of following Christ in obedient discipleship. No one was more aware of this than Edith Stein, a German Jewish philosopher who converted to Catholicism and later became a Carmelite nun. She was martyred at Auschwitz in 1942. Stein knew well the meaning of following Jesus in the way of the cross when she wrote:

> "Thy will be done," in its full extent, must be the guideline for the Christian life. It must regulate the day from morning to evening, the course of the year and the entire life. . . . All other concerns the Lord takes over. This one alone, however, remains ours as long as we live.

Stein, also known as St. Teresa Benedicta of the Cross, went on to say:

> Will you remain faithful to the Crucified? Consider carefully! The world is in flames, the battle between Christ and the Antichrist has broken into the open. If you decide for Christ, it could cost you your life. Carefully consider what you promise.[1]

Jesus began his journey to the cross with a focused resolve based on the realization of his own human mortality. He was aware of his life purpose in perspective to life's brevity and God's mission.

For us, Ash Wednesday is a sobering reminder to stay focused on life's true God purpose. Our lives, too, are short, as pointed out by the psalmist:

> Show me, LORD, my life's end
> and the number of my days;
> let me know how fleeting my life is.

You have made my days a mere handbreadth;
>the span of my years is as nothing before you.
Everyone is but a breath,
>even those who seem secure.

(Psalm 39:4-5)

I am currently in my fourth decade of ministry at Ginghamsburg Church, and this is the third church I have served since beginning as a student pastor in 1972. How did I get to be this old so quickly?

Recently at a bookstore appearance in Indianapolis, a woman approached the table where I was signing books and told me she had seen me speak at a conference twenty years ago where I had first signed a book for her. That book had a picture of me on the back cover that portrayed a much younger version prior to baldness and gray beard. She looked at me, checked the picture on the back of the twenty-year-old cover, and without thinking blurted out, "What happened?" "Time happened," I responded. We both had a great laugh!

Life on earth is not our permanent residence.

Do you remember the periodic table of elements from high school chemistry class? Everything your body is made of can be found on that chart. What a humbling thought. All the chemical elements that comprise my physical body can, in essence, be found in the dirt! This is what it means when your forehead is marked with the burnt ashes from the prior year's Palm Sunday palms. It's an important reminder of the fragile and transient nature of our time on earth. As God told Adam in the garden, "For dust you *are*, / And to dust you shall return" (Genesis 3:19 NKJV).

We must keep in the forefront of our focus that life on earth is not our permanent residence. We are here on temporary assignment. We want to be able to say on the Day of Judgment, "Mission accomplished; I have finished the work for which I was sent!"

God's Kairos Mission

The ancient Greeks had two words for time. The first word was chronos, which meant chronological or sequential time. There are 24 hours in a day, 7 days in a week, and 365 days in a year. Referring to time in the sense of chronos was quantitative in nature. The second word was *kairos*, which referred to time that was more permanent or eternal in nature—God time, so to speak. While chronos time refers to quantitative time, kairos is qualitative time.

Jesus, aware of the limited nature of his chronos time on earth, resolutely set his focus on accomplishing his kairos mission given by heaven. On Thursday evening, the night marked by his last supper with his disciples and his later arrest, we are given this account of his priorities:

> Jesus knew that the Father had put all things under his power, and that he had come from God and was returning to God; so he got up from the meal, took off his outer clothing, and wrapped a towel around his waist. After that, he poured water into a basin and began to wash his disciples' feet, drying them with the towel that was wrapped around him. (John 13:3-5)

Within the emotional tsunami of impending betrayal by those closest to him, as well as the certainty of execution for heresy charges made by the religious bureaucracy and backed by the state, this rebel of the renegade gospel chose the servant role. What an upside-down, countercultural demonstration of leadership and power contrasted against the religious and political leaders of his time and ours! In making that choice, Jesus confirmed that our life's mission lies between two points: knowing from whom we have come and to whom we will return.

Dietrich Bonhoeffer wrote concerning Jesus' forty days of temptation in the wilderness and Satan's offer to give Jesus rule over all earthly kingdoms: "Jesus could have been Lord of this world. As the Messiah the Jews had dreamed of, he could have freed Israel and led it to fame and honor. . . . He knows that for this dominion he would have to pay a price that is too high for him. It would come at the cost of obedience to God's will."[2]

Instead of accepting Satan's offer, Jesus answered, "It is written: 'Worship the Lord your God and serve him only'" (Luke 4:8). Jesus knew that unwavering obedience to God's kingdom mission would mean rejection, even from his own people, the people for whom he would give his life to save. Obedience would lead to isolation, persecution, torture, and death. This is the juncture where we begin to grasp the full meaning of Jesus' humanity. Jesus the man experienced fear, temptation to make compromises, and the doubt that he expressed fully at his execution: "My God, my God, why have you forsaken me?" (Matthew 27:46).

Following Jesus in the way of the cross means resolute commitment to fulfilling God's kairos mission, a mission that lies between the two points of knowing from whom we have come and to whom we will return.

Do You Understand What You Are Signing Up For?

In your relationships with one another, have the same mindset as Christ Jesus:

Who, being in very nature God,
    did not consider equality with God something
    to be used to his own advantage;
rather, he made himself nothing
    by taking the very nature of a servant,
    being made in human likeness.
And being found in appearance as a man,
    he humbled himself
    by becoming obedient to death—
      even death on a cross!
                (Philippians 2:5-8)

Jesus' encounters with people in the final weeks leading up to his arrest and crucifixion illuminate the meaning of the cross and the cost of following Jesus in obedient discipleship. Almost immediately after beginning his final trek from Galilee to the Holy City, Jesus encountered three different individuals. He invited all three to join him in his journey, and their responses illustrate our own confusion about what it means to be a Jesus follower.

The first man enthusiastically offered himself as a volunteer, saying, "I will follow you wherever you go" (Luke 9:57). In the man's response we see the genesis of a problem deeply rooted in the twenty-first-century church: we come to Jesus offering ourselves as volunteers rather than as servants. In my years of pastoral ministry, I have intentionally chosen not to use the word *volunteer*. Volunteers serve out of the convenience of their calendars, controlling when, where, and how they participate. They say, "I'll be there as long as I have the time, it's not too inconvenient, and it doesn't conflict with more pressing priorities (such as kids' soccer, a golf league, a dinner party, and on and on)." Volunteers follow Jesus up to a point—the point of interference with their lifestyle.

Our comfortable lifestyles are the first points of challenge that Jesus makes when we seek to join his countercultural company of the committed. He doesn't hesitate to challenge those lifestyles or the values that have become possessive idols.

In Chapter Two we discussed how easily the church can overlook Jesus' directive to take care of the poor, given the rampant "affluenza" that infects us. Can I be honest with you? I am one of those who struggle with materialism. All of us grow accustomed to the comforts that we insulate ourselves with, comforts that seem to grow with the passage of time along with a creeping sense of entitlement.

Carolyn and I were married for fourteen years before we had saved enough money to make a down payment on a house. We lived in rental or church-owned properties during those early years. Our first full-time appointment after I graduated seminary was to an exciting church in the Cincinnati area. I was the third pastor added to the staff, which meant there would be no parsonage available, so we immediately began searching for an apartment close to the church. We found a townhouse in that local area, but it wouldn't become available for almost two months after our starting date at our new assignment.

Thankfully, Mr. Merts, an elderly widower in the church, offered to house us for two months in his attic. Yes, you heard me right—in his attic! There was one old antique double bed that creaked and squeaked with the slightest movement and a small table with two mismatched chairs to share our meals on. Mr. Merts was generous in allowing us to use his kitchen and bathroom, but can you imagine how hot it was living in an attic in the Midwest during the months of June and July?

Late on a Saturday night, lying in that creaky bed before our first Sunday in the new church, I read these words of Jesus: "Foxes have dens and birds have nests, but the Son of Man has no place to lay his head" (Luke 9:58). I remember saying in a whisper just loud enough to avoid waking my wife, "Thank you, Jesus, for allowing me to participate with you in this exciting journey. I will go anywhere you send me, live in whatever state you call me to. I ask only that you take me and use me for your purpose on earth."

It is so easy to seek the gifts of God rather than the God who gives.

I continue to offer that prayer, and yet I still struggle with the conflicting values of the American dream and the kingdom of God. It is so easy to seek the gifts of God rather than the God who gives. Our expectations grow with income and age. The 36-inch color TV still works fine, but a 52-inch flatscreen is so much better, especially when expertly installed with surround sound. Materialism continues to slither forward, thanks to the engineered obsolescence of our smartphones, tablets, and laptops.

The alluring addiction of a consumerist culture bids us to come forth and indulge. The "buy now and pay later" mantra has created a massive debt load for the average American. One 2014 consumer debt service reported that the average U.S. household was carrying $15,607 in credit card debt, $153,500 in mortgage debt, and $32,656 in student loan debt.[3] We Christians have long taught the biblical principle of tithing, giving 10 percent of income to serve God's kingdom; yet we trend with the rest of the American public in giving about 2.2 percent of our personal disposable income to nonprofit groups.[4] We avoid the gospel call to give our lives sacrificially with Jesus for the world that God loves and instead use God to serve our personal interests. "Thy will be done" becomes "My will be done."

Following Jesus in the way of the cross will mean a radical reordering of our priorities. We get a glimpse of those priorities in two of Jesus' parables. In Luke 10:25-37, Jesus told the story of a good

Samaritan who sacrifices his time and financial resources to help an unknown stranger. "Go and do likewise," Jesus commanded a Jewish expert in the Law. In Luke 12:13-21, Jesus related the parable of a rich man who forgets his responsibility to be a channel for God's blessings in helping the least and the lost. The man in the story wastes his precious gift of life, living only to serve his expanding lust for bigger, better, and more. Jesus told him, " 'You fool! This very night your life will be demanded from you. Then who will get what you have prepared for yourself?' This is how it will be with whoever stores up things for themselves but is not rich toward God' " (verses 20-21). What a poignant reminder—the only thing we can take with us beyond death is what we do for God and others.

Following Jesus means relinquishing the rights to all that we are and all that we possess. When a young entrepreneur came asking how to prioritize his life, Jesus told him, "Sell everything you have and give to the poor, and you will have treasure in heaven. Then come, follow me" (Luke 18:22). When the young man heard this he walked away, choosing the comfort and security of his lifestyle over the renegade gospel of Jesus and the kingdom of God.

Following Jesus means being "rich toward God" by serving God's interests in meeting others' needs. Jesus put it this way in one of his parables: "I tell you, use worldly wealth to gain friends for yourselves, so that when it is gone, you will be welcomed into eternal dwellings" (Luke 16:9). The rebel Jesus calls us to use our affluence for the purpose of influence in the lives of people who have neither.

The season of Lent gives us an opportunity to fast not just with food but from the material distractions that we idolize. During the forty days leading up to Easter, for example, I make it a practice to purchase only such essentials as food, gas, and health supplies. And let's keep in mind that Lenten disciplines needn't be limited to the Easter season; we can practice them year-round to better align our values and priorities with the values and priorities of God's kingdom.

THE CROSS CHALLENGES THE PRIORITY OF OUR RELATIONSHIPS

Now we come to the second encounter mentioned in the Gospel of Luke immediately after Jesus began his final journey toward the fulfillment of his destiny. When Jesus said, "Follow me," the second man replied, "Lord, first let me go and bury my father." At first glance Jesus' response seems harsh and uncaring: "Let the dead bury their own dead, but you go and proclaim the kingdom of God" (Luke 9:59-60). Let's look more closely, however, at the man's reply in the context of the cultural setting.

The Jewish practice of burial lasted from twelve months to two years. The Gospel of John gives insight into the first step of the burial process after Jesus' body was taken down from the cross:

> Taking Jesus' body, the two of them wrapped it, with the spices, in strips of linen. This was in accordance with Jewish burial customs. At the place where Jesus was crucified, there was a garden, and in the garden a new tomb, in which no one had ever been laid. Because it was the Jewish day of Preparation and since the tomb was nearby, they laid Jesus there. (John 19:40-42)

Unlike the Egyptian practice of mummification and the current practice of embalming, the Jews had no intention of preserving the body. Wrapping the body in spices and placing it in a temporary tomb was only the first step in the process. The entire process could last up to two years.

There is another possibility we should mention when looking at Jesus' response to the second man. If we read carefully, we can see that it's possible the father had not yet died and that the man was anticipating the father's death and burial. In that case it was the cultural expectation that the oldest son remain and take responsibility for the final care of the father and then through the extended burial process.

In either case—whether the time period would have been up to two years or even more—Jesus was challenging the priority that we place on relationships when they become an excuse for not acting on God's will. In other words, relationships will not be considered an excuse for putting off until tomorrow what we know God is calling us to do today.

Jesus spoke more about this subject as he continued his journey to Jerusalem.

> Large crowds were traveling with Jesus, and turning to them he said: "If anyone comes to me and does not hate father and mother, wife and children, brothers and sisters—yes, even their own life—such a person cannot be my disciple. And whoever does not carry their cross and follow me cannot be my disciple." (Luke 14:25-27)

Obviously Jesus didn't really want us to hate those closest to us. But he was saying that our love and allegiance to him must supersede and take precedence over all other relationships, even those with our families. In fact, giving Jesus first priority actually makes for greater health in all our relationships, helping us build unbreakable bonds in marriage and raise healthy, God-serving children! Our children adopt the passions we demonstrate through our priorities. This might be one of the main reasons, as discussed in Chapter One, that the vast majority of young people between the ages of eighteen and thirty-five are absent from the church and why the fastest-growing religion in the United States is no religion.[5] We must rightly align our passions and priorities with our profession of faith.

Based on what I see, romantic encounters outside of marriage are one of the primary areas where seemingly sincere people who have pledged allegiance to Jesus compromise their Kingdom journey. Human beings have an incredible capacity to call wrong right, confuse lust with love, and romanticize the deep-seated lure of insecure selfishness. I can't tell you how many times I have witnessed a spiritually alive follower of Jesus become romantically entwined with a person who has little or no spiritual inclination, causing the follower to be spiritually neutralized. This is what the Apostle Paul meant when he wrote:

> Don't be tied up as equal partners with people who don't believe. What does righteousness share with that which is outside the Law? What relationship does light have with darkness? What harmony does Christ have with Satan? What does a believer have in common with someone who doesn't believe?
>
> (2 Corinthians 6:14-15 CEB)

Jesus makes it painfully clear: You cannot follow the living God in the way of the cross and serve the expectations of a spiritually dead person at the same time. You must make a choice. You must choose to serve a spiritually dead relationship or the living God. It's yet another meaning of what Jesus told the second man: you must "let the dead bury their own dead, but you go and proclaim the kingdom of God" (Luke 9:60) through the visible demonstration of your lifestyles, relationships, and calendar priorities.

THE CROSS CHALLENGES OUR INDECISIVENESS

When Jesus said, "Follow me," the third man also presented himself as a willing volunteer, saying, "I will follow you, Lord; but first let me go back and say goodbye to my family." Jesus' response made it clear that following Jesus is an all-or-nothing proposition: "No one who puts a hand to the plow and looks back is fit for service in the kingdom of God" (Luke 9:61-62). Jesus' authority, like no other religious authority that had come before him, called for an immediate response. The disciples following Jesus on his journey most surely would have recognized the difference between Jesus' reaction and that of Elijah, one of the greatest Jewish prophets, in a similar situation. They knew from Scripture what had happened when Elijah first met his future disciple Elisha:

> So Elijah departed from there and found Elisha, Shaphat's son. He was plowing with twelve yoke of oxen before him. Elisha was with the twelfth yoke. Elijah met up with him and threw his coat on him. Elisha immediately left the oxen and ran after Elijah. "Let me kiss my father and my mother," Elisha said, "then I will follow you." Elijah replied, "Go! I'm not holding you back!" (1 Kings 19:19-20 CEB)

In reacting differently from Elijah, Jesus made it pointedly clear that his authority superseded even the greatest of the Jewish prophets who had come before him and that the commitment to take up the cross demanded an immediate response. In responding to Jesus, Peter and his brother Andrew "immediately" left their nets to follow Jesus. When Jesus found his soon-to-be disciple Matthew at his place of business and called him, Matthew "got up and followed." At the bidding of Jesus, Zacchaeus the tax collector left his perch in a tree, his spectator's view from the pew, and came down "at once." As an act of repentance, Zacchaeus surrendered himself to Jesus' strategy for kingdom-of-God economics: "Look, Lord! Here and now I give half of my possessions to the poor, and if I have cheated anybody out of anything, I will pay back four times the amount" (Luke 19:8).

We claim to be followers of Jesus, yet we fail to follow.

Indecisiveness and nominalism—the practice of downplaying or denying the existence of universal truths—are two of the cancerous conditions infecting the church today and making Christianity irrelevant to the general public and especially to young adults under the age of forty. We claim to be followers of Jesus, yet we fail to follow. We profess a cross without a cost. As discussed in Chapter Two, we pledge allegiance to the rebel Jesus who has heralded the dawning of a new, countercultural community that no longer defines itself by ideologies of right or left, red or blue. Yet we have compromised Jesus' radical call to take up the cross and die to our personal prejudices and self-serving agendas. We have failed to be good news for the poor and oppressed and have forgotten God's requirement "to act justly and to love mercy and to walk humbly with your God" (Micah 6:8).

Dr. Martin Luther King, Jr., initiated the nonviolent Birmingham campaign against racism and racial segregation on April 3, 1963, eight years after leading the Montgomery public transportation strike. In the Birmingham campaign, he met resistance when a circuit judge issued a blanket injunction against parading, demonstrating, boycotting, trespassing, and picketing. King also met with sharp resistance from local clergy who argued that racial segregation shouldn't be fought through nonviolent demonstrations on the street but should be handled in the courts. King's words, written from a Birmingham jail cell, were chillingly prophetic for the church today:

> If today's church does not recapture the sacrificial spirit of the early church, it will lose its authenticity, forfeit the loyalty of millions, and be dismissed as an irrelevant social club with no meaning for the twentieth century. Every day I meet young people whose disappointment with the church has turned into outright disgust.[6]

KINGDOMS ON A COLLISION COURSE

While Jesus was heading into the Holy City from the east on the Sunday morning preceding Passover celebrations, the Roman contingent, headed by the Roman prefect Pontius Pilate, paraded into the city with quite an impressive display of military power from the west. The Romans reinforced their occupation forces on Jewish high holy days to discourage any attempted insurrection by rebel leaders who made their camps in the Galilee and wilderness regions of the country and who might take advantage of the swelling holiday crowd. Numerous political resisters had claimed to be Jewish political messiahs. They planned acts of terrorism and led rebel assaults, attempting to deliver Israel from the oppressive Roman occupation. Pilate wanted to be close enough to the Temple complex with a strong display of Roman force to ensure the "Pax Romana," Rome's version of peace. And Rome had the cross, an intimidating execution device, to enforce Roman authority with any who would question it. Thousands of criminals and perceived enemies of the state were executed along the main roads so that all could witness the penalty for insurrection.

By contrast, the rebel Jesus, who came with no sword, rode into the city on a donkey from the east with a group of ordinary working-class folks from backward rural areas. He had been born a member of an oppressed minority and then spent the first two years of his life as a refugee in Africa, escaping Herod the Great's campaign of infanticide in Bethlehem. Early in Jesus' ministry, when people had heard where he grew up, some had commented, "Nazareth! Can anything good come from there?" (John 1:46). On this day, however, the crowds lining the streets along his route into the city hailed Jesus as "the king of Israel" (John 12:13).

In addition to the contingents led by Pilate and Jesus, there was a third force at work: the compromised religious institution. The institution was controlled by a group of aristocratic elite who were no longer concerned with caring for the poor and marginalized. This religious ruling class was intent on placating Rome for the purpose of personal gain and institutional security, with no concern for God's redemptive mission of justice and righteousness in the world.

We read in the Gospel of Mark that Jesus, responding to this compromised religious institution, went to the Temple immediately after his arrival in the city on Sunday:

> On reaching Jerusalem, Jesus entered the temple courts and began driving out those who were buying and selling there. He overturned the tables of the money changers and the benches of those selling doves, and would not allow anyone to carry merchandise through the temple courts. And as he taught them, he said, "Is it not written: 'My house will be called a house of prayer for all nations'? But you have made it 'a den of robbers.'" (Mark 11:15-17)

Did you catch the inclusive *all* in Jesus' statement? *All* means "all"! Women and Gentiles were being excluded from full participation in worshiping God. The religious bureaucrats had created a corrupted, exclusionary form of the covenant that God had made with Abraham—a covenant that God had intended to become a blessing for "all peoples" (Genesis 12:3) and to make the nation of Israel a redemptive priesthood for all nations.

Three kingdoms—led by Pilate, Jesus, and the religious elite—were on a collision course. They converged in Jerusalem, and there, during the most dramatic week in human history, the eternal Lord subjected himself to the best knockout punch that evil could throw. Jesus was crucified not simply for being a religious rabbi; he was crucified for advocating a revolutionary movement that threatened the religious and political interests. Jewish leaders sought to kill him because his teachings were considered heretical.

> But Jesus said to them, "I have shown you many good works from the Father. For which of these do you stone me?" "We are not stoning you for any good work," they replied, "but for blasphemy, because you, a mere man, claim to be God." (John 10:32-33)

His growing popularity among the common people gathered in the Holy City for the Passover made him a threat to the religious hierarchy.

How do you eliminate a subversive threat? The Jewish leaders turned Jesus over to the Roman authorities, saying, "We have found this man subverting our nation. He opposes payment of taxes to Caesar and claims to be Messiah, a king" (Luke 23:2). Jesus was condemned as a heretic by the religious elite and sentenced by the Romans for the crime of political treason, for being heralded "king of the Jews" (John 19:3).

So, now that we have thought once again about that all-important week, what did Jesus mean when he gave the clear admonition that we cannot follow if we do not "take up our cross daily"?

The worship center of Ginghamsburg Church, where I have pastored for most of the last four decades, is a multipurpose space in which our folks with artistic talents create amazing, inspiring platform sets for each new worship series. Sometimes the cross is visibly present in the room, and other times it is not. When it's not, invariably a well-meaning participant will ask me how we can be a Christian place of worship without physically having a cross in the room.

I try to explain that the cross is more than just a physical object; it is a commitment to a radically different lifestyle. In Dietrich Bonhoeffer's words:

> The cross is not misfortune and hard fate. It is instead the suffering that comes to us from being bound to Jesus Christ. The cross is not accidental, but necessary suffering. The cross is not suffering bound up with natural existence, but suffering bound up with being a Christian.[7]

Following Jesus in the way of the cross means giving ourselves fully and sacrificially for the concerns of God's heart. In saying yes to Jesus, it is his cross we are lifting, his cause we are embracing, and his life mission we are supporting. Saying yes to Jesus is an all-out, all-in commitment to go where Jesus goes, be who Jesus is, do what Jesus does, and give what Jesus gives for the life of the world that God loves and gives himself for. Bonhoeffer goes on to say, "Although we are not Christ, if we want to be Christians we must participate in Christ's own magnanimous heart by engaging in responsible action that seizes the hour in complete freedom, facing the danger."[8] The Lenten journey is a forty-day, intensely focused period of personal reflection and repentance through prayer, Scripture reading, and fasting. We make a commitment sacrificially to lay aside things we ordinarily enjoy (such as sugar, alcohol, television, or social media) and to reevaluate our faith journey by asking some hard questions. Does my faith talk match my faith walk? Am I trying to live with a foot in two contradictory worlds? Am I putting off until tomorrow what God is calling me to do today? Am I offering myself to Jesus as a volunteer who serves when convenient or a servant who acts sacrificially?

We will not experience resurrection to the miracle of abundant life here on earth and life everlasting until we put to death our self-determination. As Jesus expressed it before he left for Jerusalem and the events of Holy Week:

> "Whoever wants to be my disciple must deny themselves and take up their cross daily and follow me. For whoever wants to save their life will lose it, but whoever loses their life for me will save it. What good is it for someone to gain the whole world, and yet lose or forfeit their very self?" (Luke 9:23-25)

CHAPTER SIX

RESURRECTION

CHAPTER SIX
RESURRECTION

But if it is preached that Christ has been raised from
the dead, how can some of you say that there is no
resurrection of the dead? If there is no resurrection
of the dead, then not even Christ has been raised.
And if Christ has not been raised, our preaching
is useless and so is your faith.

(1 Corinthians 15:12-14)

The most astonishing claim made by the first followers of Jesus was his physical resurrection from the grave. All claims to his messianic authority are based in this single event as a historical phenomenon. The early Christian movement was centered firmly in resurrection. Peter's sermon on the Day of Pentecost was based on the fact that "God has raised this Jesus to life, and we are all witnesses of it" (Acts 2:32). Paul's first letter to the Corinthian church, written no more than thirty years after Jesus' resurrection, testified to the event:

> For what I received I passed on to you as of first importance: that Christ died for our sins according to the Scriptures, that he was buried, that he was raised on the third day according to the Scriptures, and that he appeared to Cephas, and then to the Twelve. After that, he appeared to more than five hundred of the brothers and sisters at the same time, most of whom are still living, though some have fallen asleep.
>
> (1 Corinthians 15:3-6)

The embryonic revolutionary movement brought early persecution to its members. The priests and Temple guard "were greatly disturbed because the apostles were teaching the people, proclaiming in Jesus the resurrection of the dead" (Acts 4:2). The Resurrection was the central, repetitive, core theme as the gospel movement spread beyond Palestine. We read that Paul's sermon thesis in the Jewish synagogue in Thessalonica was based on "explaining and proving that the Messiah had to suffer and rise from the dead. 'This Jesus I am proclaiming to you is the Messiah,' he said" (Acts 17:3). We find the Athenians reacting in a questioning manner to Paul's message: "A group of Epicurean and Stoic philosophers began to debate with him. Some of them asked, 'What is this babbler trying to say?' Others remarked, 'He seems to be advocating foreign gods.' They said this because Paul was preaching the good news about Jesus and the resurrection" (Acts 17:18).

The renegade gospel movement began to create revolutionary tension as it spread throughout the Roman Empire, because its followers were "all defying Caesar's decrees, saying that there is another king, one called Jesus" (Acts 17:7). The firm belief of Jesus' early followers that God had acted in a unique way through the bodily resurrection of Jesus confirmed his identity as the Messiah. More than anything else in Jesus' life, ministry, or teaching, this one event fueled the movement's rapid spread. British theologian N. T. Wright has stated:

> Take away the stories of Jesus's birth, and you lose only two chapters of Matthew and two of Luke. Take away the resurrection, and you lose the entire New Testament and most of the second-century fathers as well.[1]

I Believe; Help My Unbelief

The resurrection of Jesus is the story I have bet my life on. The Resurrection has defined my life direction and priorities since I said yes to Jesus' invitation to follow over four decades ago. I have experienced the transforming power of the resurrection in my own life. Yet I have a confession to make: I still struggle with doubt.

I have always been able to relate to the biblical account in the Gospel of Mark where a man asked Jesus to help his son, who was experiencing an affliction resulting in life-threatening convulsions:

> Jesus asked the boy's father, "How long has he been like this?"

> "From childhood," he answered. "It has often thrown him into fire or water to kill him. But if you can do anything, take pity on us and help us."

> "'If you can'?" said Jesus. "Everything is possible for one who believes."

Immediately the boy's father exclaimed, "I do believe;
help me overcome my unbelief!" (Mark 9:21-24)

The father's confession that he has both faith and doubt at
the same time expresses the tension in my own faith journey.
"I believe; help my unbelief" has become my daily prayer mantra
as I move forward, called to finish the work of God for which I
was created.

This faith-doubt struggle seems to have been normative for
many of Jesus' first disciples. We are told in Matthew's Gospel
that, following the Resurrection, "the eleven disciples went to
Galilee, to the mountain where Jesus had told them to go.
When they saw him, they worshiped him; but some doubted"
(Matthew 28:16-17). We read in Luke's account that Jesus appeared
to the disciples, who had barricaded themselves behind locked
doors fearing the authorities' retribution after witnessing the
execution of the one they believed to be Israel's deliverer. "Why are
you troubled, and why do doubts rise in your minds? Look at my
hands and my feet. It is I myself! Touch me and see; a ghost does
not have flesh and bones, as you see I have" (Luke 24:38-39). Even
when witnessing the Resurrection miracle, the disciples struggled
with doubt!

Even Jesus experienced dark nights of the soul.

Great servants of Jesus' movement have continued to struggle
with the same issues of faith. In the book *Come Be My Light*,
which contains Mother Teresa's correspondence with her spiritual
directors, we get a glimpse into her own struggles of faith and
sense of abandonment by God. She wrote, "My own soul remains
in deep darkness and desolation. . . . As for me—the silence and

the emptiness is so great that I look and do not see, listen and do not hear." This humble servant of Christ experienced an intense faith-doubt struggle for forty years. Mother Teresa, however, didn't allow doubt to be the paralyzing factor in her faith journey: "I don't complain—let Him do with me whatever He wants."[2] You and I are not alone in this faith-doubt struggle. The Resurrection challenges the paradigm of our possibilities, even for Mother Teresa. Sometimes people in my church tell me that they wish they had the faith that I have. I don't have a tremendous amount of faith. Like you, I struggle with the battle between heart and mind. It's not that some people have faith and no doubt and others have doubt and no faith. Faith and doubt seem to go together. I would love to have the faith of Jesus. But even Jesus experienced dark nights of the soul. In the Gospel of Mark we read the last words uttered by Jesus on the cross: "My God, my God, why have you forsaken me?" (Mark 15:34).

MUSTARD SEED FAITH

The disciples asked Jesus to increase their faith. Jesus reminded them that an abundance of faith is not necessary: "If you have faith as small as a mustard seed, you can say to this mulberry tree, 'Be uprooted and planted in the sea,' and it will obey you" (Luke 17:6). So it's not about how much faith you have, but how much of what you have that you commit to action. The Resurrection defines the new possible—just as Jesus responded to the man who asked Jesus if he could help his son, "Everything is possible for one who believes" (Mark 9:23).

Resurrection faith begins with a renewed way of thinking. Before you can be raised to a new level of life, you have to die to old ways of thinking. You have to have new life pictures! This means releasing past assumptions, feelings, and practices.

Resurrection thinking affects every area of our lives. From our relationships to the way we think about the stewardship of time and financial resources, we must die to old patterns of thinking and be raised to the new. What is the new reality? Things that are impossible for human beings are possible for God. Ask yourself: "What can God do through me if I am willing to risk acting on the mustard seed faith that I have?" The impossible is the new possible!

People who defy conventional wisdom are often the ones who contribute the most to human advancement. Some of the best scientific minds of the fifteenth century were convinced the earth was flat. As a result, folks thought Christopher Columbus was crazy! Do you think that when Columbus set sail on August 3, 1492, he knew for an absolute fact the earth was round? Surely he doubted. But Columbus didn't allow those doubts to override his conviction to act on the "things not yet seen." With the example of Columbus in mind, I recommend taking some time to reflect on the meaning of faith as described in the Letter to the Hebrews: "Now faith is confidence in what we hope for and assurance about what we do not see" (11:1).

In the 1950s, scientists were still debating the possibility of moon travel. Then the Russians launched the first satellite, Sputnik 1, in 1957. On May 25, 1961, President John F. Kennedy announced before a joint session of Congress the ambitious goal of landing an American on the moon by the end of the decade. Crazy? Impossible? Unrealistic? The American spacecraft Apollo 11 landed the first humans on the moon on July 20, 1969.

People believed it was impossible for the human body to break the threshold of four minutes in running one mile—that is, until Roger Bannister did it in 1954 with a time of 3:59.4. The barrier that had stood for centuries is now broken regularly. What was considered undoable is now doable! For the impossible to become possible, you must believe it is possible; you must believe it before you can achieve it. To be raised to a new way of living, you have to die to an old way of thinking.

I came to Ginghamsburg Church in 1979 when it was just a little chapel built in 1876, in a village of twenty-two houses with fewer than one hundred people in the congregation. The Miami Valley region of Ohio, where the church is located, has declined in population during my almost four decades of ministry here. Human reasoning would have indicated that it was impossible to grow a successful church here. But Ginghamsburg Church has helped thousands throughout the area. It has partnered with local government agencies to build low-income housing in at-risk neighborhoods in the city of Dayton, as well as 269 schools in the Darfur region of the Sudan involving over 32,000 students.

I have often shared the story about taking a whole day when I arrived in 1979 to dream God's dream for Ginghamsburg. Such times of visioning are absolutely essential for fertilizing the mustard seeds of Resurrection faith. I remember sharing the vision that God had given me with my supervisor (district superintendent). I told him I could see the day when three thousand people would worship at Ginghamsburg. The church would demonstrate racial and economic diversity. Our mission would be to grow disciples of Jesus who would demonstrate the kingdom of God on earth. Needless to say, my district superintendent thought I was crazy, even though he used the nicer term "naïve"! He reminded me that up to that time there had never been a United Methodist Church in Ohio that had been larger than twelve hundred in worship attendance. To be raised to a new way of living, you have to die to an old way of thinking. For the impossible to become possible, you have to believe it is possible!

Correlating Resurrection Faith and Life Outcomes

Capernaum is called the town of Jesus. In biblical times it was a fishing village located on the northern corner of the Sea of Galilee. The town was Jesus' headquarters for most of the three years of his public ministry. It was where he met and called his first disciples, only later to be considered renegade rebels. Jesus met his disciples on the beach there for a breakfast "barbecue" shortly after his resurrection.

Most of the miracles reported in the Gospels took place in the area of Capernaum. In Matthew 9:27-33, we read the accounts of three people who experienced healing through Jesus' ministry. Two were blind men following Jesus through the town pleading for his merciful touch. Jesus asked them, " 'Do you believe that I am able to do this?' 'Yes, Lord,' they replied." Now, notice what Jesus did in response to the men's expression of faith: "Then he touched their eyes and said, 'According to your faith let it be done to you'; and their sight was restored" (verses 28-30).

We experience God's presence and healing power in proportion to the level of faith we already have and act upon. "I believe; help my unbelief." It doesn't take much; you only need faith the size of a mustard seed! But faith is more than just being transformed in our thinking about the new possible. The Bible reminds us that we also need to be transformed in our actions.

The Epistle of James is one of my most underlined sections in the Bible, partly because James has so much to say about our faith and our actions:

> Do not merely listen to the word, and so deceive your-
> selves. Do what it says. (1:22)

What good is it, my brothers and sisters, if someone claims to have faith but has no deeds? Can such faith save them? Suppose a brother or a sister is without clothes and daily food. If one of you says to them, "Go in peace; keep warm and well fed," but does nothing about their physical needs, what good is it? In the same way, faith by itself, if it is not accompanied by action, is dead. (2:14-17)

Show me your faith without deeds, and I will show you my faith by my deeds. You believe that there is one God. Good! Even the demons believe that—and shudder." (2:18-19)

And then the author breaks down the crux of Resurrection faith to the lowest common denominator:

You see that a person is considered righteous by what they do and not by faith alone (2: 24).

Throughout the New Testament, faith is activated through the commitment of physical movement. The messenger told the women at the tomb to *go* and *tell* the disciples and Peter (Mark 16:7). When the women shared their discovery with the disciples, Peter didn't sit back crossing his arms waiting to be convinced; he *ran* to the tomb to *see* for himself (John 20:4). Faith is movement! Faith is action! Faith is always moving toward a desired outcome.

DEALING WITH DOUBT

In Luke's account of the first Easter day, Jesus suddenly appeared in the group of his disciples later in the evening. Luke describes the disciples' response: "They were startled and frightened, thinking they saw a ghost" (24:37). That passage is probably a bit understated; I daresay there was the smell of panic and confusion in the room. It is also worth noting that the disciples still experienced doubt even when the physical evidence was standing right before their eyes.

Jesus asked his startled disciples a question that continues to be extremely relevant for us today: "Why are you troubled, and why do doubts rise in your minds?" (24:38). I can tell you why. Resurrections are not rational! Yet, on the basis of this illogical claim, the illegal renegade movement spread rapidly through the Roman Empire. And in spite of persecutions, the movement continues to grow.

The Pew Forum on Religion and Public Life co-hosted a meeting with the Council on Foreign Relations in March of 2005 to address the rapid spread of Christianity in today's developing world. The Pew Forum issued a paper afterward highlighting the findings of the meeting, titled "Faith and Conflict: The Global Rise of Christianity." The introduction to the paper noted, "With more than two billion adherents worldwide, Christianity is both the world's largest and, in some regions, its fastest growing religion, with most of that growth taking place in the developing world." In the paper itself, Professor Mark Noll of Wheaton College went on to support the assertion:

> In order to grasp the current situation of world Christianity concretely, consider what went on last Sunday. More Roman Catholics attended church in the Philippines than in any single country of Europe. In China, where in 1970 there were no legally functioning churches at all, more believers probably gathered for worship than in all of so-called "Christian Europe." . . .

In Korea, where a century ago there existed only a bare handful of Christian believers, more people attended the Yoido Full Gospel Church in Seoul than all of the churches in significant American denominations like the Christian Reformed Church."[3]

Is it possible, as suggested in Chapter One, that Resurrection faith is better fertilized in places where people face persecution and struggle? Perhaps that is what the Apostle Paul meant when he wrote, " I want to know Christ—yes, to know the power of his resurrection and participation in his sufferings, becoming like him in his death, and so, somehow, attaining to the resurrection from the dead" (Philippians 3:10-11).

I worship the resurrected Christ and deal with doubts at the same time. How about you?

Like the disciples who experienced Jesus' post-Resurrection appearance in Galilee, I worship the resurrected Christ and deal with doubts at the same time. How about you?

Jesus asked, "Why are you troubled, and why do doubts rise in your minds?" In the very next sentence, Jesus' instructed the troubled disciples using three active verbs: "*Look* at my hands and my feet. It is I myself! *Touch* me and *see*; a ghost does not have flesh and bones, as you see I have" (Luke 24:38-39, emphasis added). There is no doubt that the author was referring to a literal, physical event.

N. T. Wright points out that Jesus appears in the post-Resurrection Gospel accounts "as a human being with a body that in some ways is quite normal and can be mistaken for a gardener or a fellow traveler on the road."[4] Wright goes on to state,

"Belief in bodily resurrection was one of the two central things that the pagan doctor Galen noted about the Christians (the other being their remarkable sexual restraint)."[5]

LOOK—AT THE CREDIBLE EVIDENCE

In the Luke passage above, the first directive Jesus gave his disciples was to look at the physical evidence: "Look at my hands and feet."

We first must ask ourselves, does the Resurrection have historical credibility? Keep in mind that historical evidence is different from scientific evidence in the sense that it can't be reproduced in a laboratory to prove its validity. Does Ivory soap float as its commercials used to claim? You can easily test the premise by dropping ten bars of Ivory soap into a tub of water. It floats! Proving the credibility of historical claims, however, is a very different matter. Did George Washington chop down a cherry tree or, later, cross the Delaware River on a December night in 1776 during the American Revolutionary War? What is fact and what is fiction? The reliability of historical evidence is tied entirely to the credibility of the contemporary witnesses and the number of witnesses at the time of the occurrence.

The Apostle Paul's first letter to the Corinthian church is usually dated in the range of A.D. 53 to 57, less than thirty years after Jesus' reported resurrection. In the fifteenth chapter Paul makes the claim that Jesus physically appeared to the twelve, and "after that, he appeared to more than five hundred of the brothers and sisters at the same time, most of who are still living, though some have fallen asleep" (1 Corinthians 15:6). Many of the eyewitnesses were still living at the time this letter was being broadly circulated throughout the church.

Investigative reporters are always trying to check their story with as many reliable sources as possible. The American actor and comedian John Belushi, best known for his work on the television program *Saturday Night Live* and in the movie *Animal House*, died in 1982. Jim Henson, the puppeteer who created the Muppet characters and became famous when he joined *Sesame Street* in the 1970s, died in 1990. It would be absurd to assume that a media source reporting that one of them had been raised from the dead would have any chance of credible circulation, in a relatively concentrated geographical area, witnessed by more than five hundred folk. Too many of us are alive who would refute the claim. Yet this is exactly the time frame in which the Resurrection was being reported as factual during the lifespan of hundreds of eyewitnesses.

We must also consider the countless testimonies of credible witnesses throughout the last two millennia who have claimed life-transforming experiences by encountering the risen Christ. A prime example was the radical conversion of Augustine of Hippo, better known as St. Augustine (A.D. 354-430). Perhaps no one had as much influence on Western Christian thought and theology. Augustine lived a hedonistic lifestyle before his conversion. As described in his autobiographical work *Confessions*, he had relationships with multiple women and admitted to having concubines before his life-transforming experience. Augustine explained his conversion as being prompted by a childlike voice telling him to "take up and read," which he understood to be a divine command to read the Bible. Augustine opened the Bible to Romans 13:13-14: "Let us behave decently, as in the daytime, not in carousing and drunkenness, not in sexual immorality and debauchery, not in dissension and jealousy. Rather, clothe yourselves with the Lord Jesus Christ, and do not think about how to gratify the desires of the flesh."

Sallie McFague, former Dean of Vanderbilt Divinity School, describes Augustine's change: "He is like the folks in the parables, one of us; lustful, ambitious, skeptical, gluttonous and petty. And in the midst of this realistic story, he traces the surprising ways of God, disrupting, subverting, and finally overturning his little world."[6]

The French mathematician and physicist Blaise Pascal claimed that he experienced transforming conversion on November 23, 1654, as the result of a vision of the crucifixion. "From about haft-past ten in the evening until about half-past twelve . . . FIRE . . . God of Abraham, the God of Isaac, the God of Jacob, and not of the philosophers and savants. Certitude. Certitude. Feeling. Joy. Peace." He recorded the experience on a piece of parchment, sewed it into the lining of his coat, and carried it with him the rest of his life.[7]

Many skeptics have discovered new life meaning through a relationship with the risen Christ.

Like the Apostle Paul on the road to Damascus, many skeptics have discovered new life meaning through a relationship with the risen Christ. C. S. Lewis, the British scholar, described himself as an atheist. One night he climbed into the sidecar of a friend's motorcycle for a trip to a local zoo. He later wrote, "When we set out I did not believe that Jesus is the Son of God, and when we reached the zoo I did."[8] Credible people from all walks of life continue to make the same discovery.

"Look at my hands and my feet," Jesus told the disciples. "It is I myself!"

Touch—Invitation to Involvement

In the Luke passage, Jesus' further response was inviting his startled friends to "touch me and see" (Luke 24:39). This invitation has deeper significance if we understand the context. When Jesus celebrated the Passover the evening of his arrest, he made a promise to the disciples:

> "If you love me, keep my commands. And I will ask the Father, and he will give you another advocate to help you and be with you forever—the Spirit of truth. The world cannot accept him, because it neither sees him nor knows him. But you know him, for he lives with you and will be in you. I will not leave you as orphans; I will come to you. Before long, the world will not see me anymore, but you will see me. Because I live, you also will live. On that day you will realize that I am in my Father, and you are in me, and I am in you."
>
> (John 14:15-20)

Luke gives his account of the Easter evening meeting and then moves abruptly to Jesus' ascension, skipping over the meetings in Galilee between Resurrection and Ascension that are mentioned in other Gospels. But before describing the Ascension, he quotes Jesus' final instruction: "I am going to send you what my Father has promised; but stay in the city until you have been clothed with power from on high" (Luke 24:49).

The resurrected Jesus revealed himself to his followers in a very personal and real way. But he made it clear that it's impossible to know him apart from the commitment to become intimately involved in his life and mission. Intentional participation in his life and mission is part and parcel of faith. Faith is a verb! Scientist Francis Collins described his transition from atheism to faith in a PBS interview:

> It took me a while to get comfortable sharing this experience with other people in science. I was happy to talk about it with my family and with other people who were not in the scientific arena. But like most scientists, I had this fear that having accepted something in the way of a spiritual worldview, I would be perceived as having gone just a little bit soft; that this was not compatible with the rigorous "show me the data" attitude that a scientist is supposed to have towards all things.
>
> Now, I might say that particular conclusion is, itself, all wrong. There will never be a scientific proof of God's existence. Science explores the natural, and God is outside the natural. So there is going to be no substitute for making a decision to believe, and that decision will never be undergirded by absolute data-driven proof.[9]

You cannot sit idly by waiting for scientific proof. "Touch me and see." Intentional participation in Jesus' life and mission precedes growing faith!

SEE—THROUGH THE EYES OF THE RESURRECTED CHRIST

After I encountered the resurrected rebel Jesus, he gave me new eyes with which to see. I identify with the blind man Jesus healed on the sabbath in John 9, which caused consternation among the self-righteously religious Pharisees. When the healed man was brought before the religious authorities for questioning, he defiantly declared in verse 25: "One thing I do know. I was blind but now I see!" I, too, was once blind and now I see. I am a firsthand witness to the power of the resurrected Christ as I assess how he has transformed the way I see myself and others.

Before Jesus, I defined myself by my limitations. I remember telling my parents on more than one occasion about my academic struggles, "I can't help it. I'm stupid." Once I met the resurrected Jesus, however, I felt reassured that I was God's masterpiece, created new in Christ Jesus so I could "do the good things he planned for us long ago" (Ephesians 2:10 NLT). I could now embrace the promise of Jeremiah 29:11-13:

> "For I know the plans I have for you," declares the LORD, "plans to prosper you and not to harm you, plans to give you hope and a future. Then you will call on me and come and pray to me, and I will listen to you. You will seek me and find me when you seek me with all your heart."

That doesn't mean I am completely free of self-doubt. There are moments when I struggle, times I question. Yet, as Ginghamsburg Church's Next Step Recovery community reminds me in worship each Saturday night, "I can do all this through him who gives me strength" (Philippians 4:13).

An encounter with the resurrected Jesus, however, doesn't just transform the way we view ourselves; it causes us to see others in a new light. The poor are no longer lazy, ignorant, or simply unlucky; they are the people God loves, so much so that more than two thousand Scriptures are dedicated to justice for the vulnerable and poor, the widow and orphan. God teaches us to love ourselves and love others as ourselves; the resurrected Jesus reveals that it truly is more blessed to give than to receive, and that ultimately the measure of our lives will be based on whatever we do for the least and the lost. Jesus even redefines *enemy*, not as someone to hate but as someone worth praying for, an individual of sacred worth and God-potential. Our encounters with the resurrected Jesus give us new eyes and a new resurrection worldview. With the rebel Jesus, the impossible becomes possible.

I invite you to say this prayer with me:

> Lord, by no means do I fully comprehend who you are. But I commit today to give my life to you . . . not just in words, but in action. With all my imperfections, I accept your love and forgiveness, and I extend it to others. I pledge my allegiance to the rebel Jesus and commit myself to the renegade gospel. Not my will but your will be done. In Jesus' name. Amen.

Notes

Introduction

1. Hauerwas, Stanley and William H. Willimon, *Resident Aliens: Life in the Christian Colony* (Nashville: Abingdon Press, 2008), 55.

Chapter One: Discovering the Rebel Jesus

1. Campolo,Tony, *Red Letter Christians: A Citizen's Guide to Faith and Politics* (Ventura, CA: Regal, 2008).
2. Kelly, Walt, *Pogo: We Have Met the Enemy and He Is Us* (New York: Simon & Schuster, 1987).
3. "'Nones' on the Rise," http://www.pewforum.org/2012/10/09/nones-on-the-rise.
4. Spurgeon, Charles, http://www.christianfaith.com/christian-quotes/.
5. Sitkoff, Harvard, *King: Pilgrimage to the Mountaintop* (New York: Hill and Wang, 2008), 208.

Chapter Two: Revolutionary Lifestyle

1. http://usatoday30.usatoday.com/news/religion/story/2012-05-12/church-mothers-day/54889418/1.
2. http://www.christiancentury.org/article/2011-10/why-do-men-stay-away.
3. Frost, Michael and Alan Hirsch, *ReJesus: A Wild Messiah for a Missional Church* (Ada, MI: Baker Books, 2008), 21.
4. Bonhoeffer, Dietrich, *God Is on the Cross: Reflections on Lent and Easter* (Louisville, KY: Westminster John Knox Press: 2012), editor's preface, ix.
5. http://www.ushmm.org/information/exhibitions/online-features/special-focus/dietrich-bonhoeffer.
6. http://hirr.hartsem.edu/research/fastfacts/fast_facts.html.
7. Slaughter, Michael, *Spiritual Entrepreneurs: 6 Principles for Risking Renewal* (Nashville: Abingdon Press: 1996), 42.

CHAPTER THREE: THE MOST IMPORTANT QUESTION YOU WILL EVER HAVE TO ANSWER

1. Lois Tverberg, "Covered in the Dust of Your Rabbi," January 27, 2012. http://ourrabbijesus.com/2012/01/27/covered-in-the-dust-of-your-rabbi -an-urban-legend/.
2. Strobel, Lee, *The Case for Christ: A Journalist's Personal Investigation of the Evidence for Jesus* (Grand Rapids, MI: Zondervan, 1998), 105.
3. *Pliny, Letters,* transl. by William Melmoth, rev. by W. M. L. Hutchinson (Cambridge: Harvard University Press, 1935), II, X: 96.
4. The Holy Qur'an, transl. by Maulana Muhammad Ali (Dublin, OH: Ahmadiyya Anjuman Isha'at Islam Lahore Inc., USA, 2002).
5. http://www.monticello.org/site/research-and-collections/jeffersons -religious-beliefs.
6. Lewis, C. S., *Mere Christianity* (New York: HarperCollins, 1952, renewed 1980), 53.
7. Strobel, *The Case for Christ.*
8. Collins, Francis S., *The Language of God: A Scientist Presents Evidence for Belief* (New York: Free Press, 2006), 3.
9. Wallis, Jim, *The Call to Conversion: Why Faith Is Always Personal but Never Private* (San Francisco: HarperSanFrancisco, copyright 1981, revised 2005), 78.
10. Sayers, Dorothy L., *Christian Letters to a Post-Christian World: A Selection of Essays* (Grand Rapids, MI: William B Eerdmans Publishing Company, 1969), 14.
11. "The Apostles' Creed, Traditional Version,"*The United Methodist Hymnal* (Nashville: The United Methodist Publishing House, 1989), 881.

CHAPTER FOUR: SEEING JESUS TODAY

1. http://www.christiancentury.org/article/2013-05/sticky-faith.
2. *Mary and Martha,* HBO Films, 2013.
3. *Bruce Almighty,* Universal Studios, 2003; http://www.imdb.com/title /tt0315327/quotes.
4. *The Huffington Post,* December 2013; http://www.huffingtonpost.com /2013/12/03/sleep-deprivation-accidents-disasters_n_4380349.html ?view=print&comm_ref=false.
5. "Sleep Habits: More Important than You Think; http://www.webmd.com /sleep-disorders/features/important-sleep-habits.

CHAPTER FIVE: THE WAY OF THE CROSS

1. *Edith Stein: Essential Writings* (Maryknoll, NY: Orbis Books, 2002), 125, 132.
2. Bonhoeffer, Dietrich, *God Is on the Cross: Reflections on Lent and Easter* (Louisville, KY: Westminster John Knox Press, 2012), 20.

3. "American Household Credit Card Statistics: 2014," http://www. nerdwallet.com/blog/credit-card-data/average-credit-card-debt -household/ accessed Sept. 15, 2014.

4. "How Much to Donate? God Knows," by Ron Lieber, *The New York Times*, April 30, 2010; http://www.nytimes.com/2010/05/01/your -money/01money.html?_r=0.

5. "The Religious None: A Profile of the Fast-Growing Religiously Unaffiliated," by Lauren Markoe, *Huffington Post*, October 10, 2012; http://www.huffingtonpost.com/2012/10/10/the-religious-none-a -profile_n_1952794.html.

6. King, Martin Luther, Jr., "Letter from Birmingham Jail," http://mlk-kpp01. stanford.edu/index.php/resources/article/annotated_letter_from _birmingham/.

7. Bonhoeffer, 22.

8. Ibid., 41.

CHAPTER SIX: RESURRECTION

1. Wright, N. T., *Surprised by Hope: Rethinking Heaven, the Resurrection, and the Mission of the Church* (New York: HarperOne, 2008), 43.

2 . Mother Teresa and Brian Kolodiejchuk, *Mother Teresa: Come Be My Light: The Private Writings of the Saint of Calcutta* (New York: Image, 2007), 154, 288.

3. "Faith and Conflict: The Global Rise of Christianity," Pew Research: Religion and Public Life Project (New York: Council on Foreign Relations: transcript March 2, 2005); http://www.pewforum.org /2005/03/02/faith-and-conflict-the-global-rise-of-christianity.

4. Wright, 55.

5. Ibid., 43.

6. McFague, Sallie, "Conversion: Life on the Edge of the Raft," in *Interpretation* 32.03 (ATLA Serials, 2001), 262.

7. Christian History.net. "Blaise Pascal: Scientific and Spiritual Prodigy"; posted 8/8/08 12:56PM; http://www.christianitytoday.com /ch/131christians/evangelistsandapologists/pascal.html.

8. Beliefnet. "C. S. Lewis: The Reluctant Convert," Frederica Mathewes-Green, http://www.beliefnet.com/Entertainment/Movies/Narnia /C-S-Lewis-The-Reluctant-Convert.aspx.

9. http://www.pbs.org/wgbh/questionofgod/voices/collins.html.

MIKE SLAUGHTER is a catalyst for change in the worldwide church. His dynamic teaching, heart for the lost, and innovative approach to ministry have led Ginghamsburg Church to outgrow all paradigms for a church in a cornfield. Mike's call to afflict the comfortable and comfort the afflicted will challenge all those he encounters to wrestle with God and their God-destinies.

Mike is in his fourth decade as Chief Dreamer at Ginghamsburg Church. His lifelong passion to reach the lost and set the oppressed free has made him a tireless and leading advocate for the children, women, and men of Darfur, Sudan, which was named by the United Nations as the worst humanitarian crisis in the world.

Since initiating the Sudan Project in January 2005, Ginghamsburg Church has invested nearly $7 million into humanitarian relief in Darfur. The resulting agricultural project, child development program, and safe water initiative are expanding to reach a quarter million Sudanese refugees and villagers. Mike has traveled three times to the displaced-persons camps and villages in South Darfur, and through the Sudan Project has witnessed firsthand God's "loaves and fishes" miracle, reconfirming for the Sudanese people Ginghamsburg's determined commitment to helping them.

The church was nationally recognized for its relief efforts in New Orleans following Hurricane Katrina, garnering a front page cover story in *The Times-Picayune* and articles in the *Houston Chronicle* and *Washington Post*. Since Katrina hit, the church has sent 75 teams to the city to assist in rebuilding efforts.

Photo courtesy of Ginghamsburg Church

Locally, the New Path outreach arm of Ginghamsburg Church annually serves more than 40,000 people in surrounding communities via its food pantry, car, clothing, and furniture ministries. The Clubhouse (Dreambuilders) After-School Ministry has seven Dayton-area locations where more than 400 trained teenagers each year tutor, mentor, and play with at-risk children, providing safe and educational alternatives to children being home alone after school or during summer break. The Clubhouse program was awarded a Point of Light award from President George H. W. Bush and the Presidential Voluntary Action Award from President Bill Clinton, among dozens of other national awards.

As a mentor, Mike travels globally to speak and uses his "gift of irritation" to equip ministry leaders to minimize brick and maximize mission so they may fully deploy the mission of Jesus into the world. He is the author of many books, most recently *Dare to Dream: Creating a God-Sized Mission Statement for Your Life*; *shiny gods: Finding Freedom from Things That Distract Us*; *Hijacked: Responding to the Partisan Church Divide*; *Christmas Is Not Your Birthday*; and *Change the World: Recovering the Message and Mission of Jesus*, all published by Abingdon Press.

In 2005 and 2006, *The Church Report* named Ginghamsburg one of the top 50 churches in the U.S. and in 2007 listed Mike as one of the 50 most influential Christians in America.

Mike lives in Tipp City, Ohio, with his wife Carolyn. Their children are daughter Kristen (Slaughter) Leavitt and her husband Brendan, as well as son Jonathan with wife Stacy. Mike and Carolyn have three grandchildren: Ellie, Addison, Anna, Luke, and Caleb.

**For more information or to catch up with Mike,
go to www.mikeslaughter.com.**

Dare to Dream

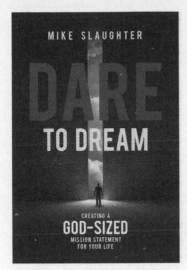

Dare to Dream is a startling and inspiring new book that draws on the Bible and a lifetime of ministry to help us discern God's dream for us and learn to live it out prayerfully and enthusiastically.

The series includes videos and readings for each week, with directed questions for discovering and creating your life mission statement. The six-week study contains a complete family of resources for the entire church.

Book
ISBN 978-1-4267-7577-2

Youth DVD
ISBN 978-1-4267-7582-6

DVD
ISBN 978-1-4267-7578-9

Youth Book
ISBN 978-1-4267-7580-2

Leader Guide
ISBN 978-1-4267-7579-6

Preview Book
ISBN 978-1-4267-7583-3

Children's Leader Guide
ISBN 978-1-4267-7581-9

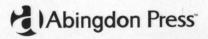